The Great Pyramid

Other books by N. W. Hutchings

Exploring the Book of Daniel
The Persian Gulf Crisis
Petra in History and Prophecy
Problem Prophetic Passages: The Olivet Discourse
The Revived Roman Empire and the Beast of the Apocalypse
Romance of Romans
Studies in Timothy
Why So Many Churches?

The Great Pyramid

Prophecy in Stone

N. W. Hutchings

THE GREAT PYRAMID: PROPHECY IN STONE

Copyright © 1996 by N. W. Hutchings

All photographs were taken by Southwest Radio Church staff photographers except those taken from Corel Professional Photos (*)

Printed in the United States of America

Table of Contents

Introduction

Anyone who dares to enter the field of Egyptology, and in particular studies relating to the Sphinx and the Great Pyramid, enters the quagmire of controversy.

Astrologers, Masons, the Illuminati, New Agers, fortune tellers, mystics, and a host of other occultists and one-world (or Babel) proponents have latched onto the Sphinx and the Great Pyramid as some kind of symbols for their cause. Satan always attempts to subvert or counterfeit.

Charlton Heston, media personalities, archaeologists and/or scientists, have presented exhaustive television programs delving into the questions and possibilities related to the age in which the pyramids of Egypt were built and how they were constructed. There is no consensus about either subject.

Among those who have proposed that the Great Pyramid was related to a Divine purpose are: Josephus, John Graves, Sir Isaac Newton, John Taylor, Astronomer Royal C. Piazzi Smyth, Dr. J. A. Seiss, J. Ralston Skinner, David Davidson, and James and Adam Rutherford. Some of the preceding have used the Great Pyramid as a base to peddle their own particular brand of theology. However, others, like Dr. Seiss, have been serious students of the Bible and great men of God.

Josephus indicated that the Great Pyramid was built by the descendants of Seth as a repository for knowledge of the heavens and a prophetic calendar. Jeremiah and Isaiah, we believe, alluded to the Great Pyramid as a testimony in stone to the Lord. In this little volume we profess to be within the limits of exegesis credibility in our humble efforts to shed some light on the most mysterious structure erected by man upon Planet Earth.

Chapter One

Wonders of the Ancient World

> Great in counsel, and mighty in work: for thine eyes are open upon
> all the ways of the sons of men: to give every one according to his
> ways, and according to the fruit of his doings: Which hast set signs
> and **wonders in the land of Egypt,** even unto this day . . . (Jer.
> 32:19–20).

The wonders of God enumerated in the Scriptures are countless
and beyond comprehension. Everything we see and touch was
created by God. Life in every form is a wonder. Man, who was
created in the image of God, may bring forth wonders limited
to three dimensions like the Tower of Babel. But even in some
of the so-called physical wonders of man, God's presence is made
known, as in the wonders of Egypt.

Man in his own wisdom has catalogued the greatest seven
wonders of man that existed in the ancient world. By the ancient world, we set this era as being the time before Christ was
born. Some recognized authorities on such matters disagree as
to which are the greatest seven man-made wonders of the ancient world. However, all agree that the Great Pyramid of Giza is
the greatest wonder of man's accomplishment. The Seven Wonders in order of their importance, as determined by the *World
Almanac,* are as follows:

1. Great Pyramid of Giza (2800–2550 B.C.)

2. Hanging Gardens of Babylon (600 B.C.)
3. Statue of Zeus (Jupiter) at Olympia
4. Colossus of Rhodes (1100 B.C.)
5. Temple of Artemis (Diana) at Ephesus (550 B.C.)
6. The Mausoleum at Halicarnassus (353 B.C.)
7. The Pharos (Lighthouse) of Alexandria (270 B.C..)

The "Seven Wonders of the Ancient World" list by the *Encyclopaedia Britannica,* based upon that proposed by Antipater of Sidon in the second century B.C., corresponds with the one in the *World Almanac,* with the exception that the Hanging Gardens are called the Gardens of Semiramis, and coequal with the Lighthouse of Alexandria, Egypt, are the Walls of Babylon. Even the sages of the ages agree with the prophet, Jeremiah, that God has established wonders in Egypt, as three of the seven wonders are within the boundaries of this nation.

Considering the Seven Wonders of the Ancient World in reverse order we have:

7. **Pharos Lighthouse of Alexandria**—The city of Alexandria was named in memory of Alexander the Great, who defeated the Persian army and extended his empire from Greece to Libya to India. There are many cities in northeast Africa, Asia Minor, and southwest Asia named Alexandria. The island of Pharos is located at the entrance to the harbor of Alexandria. To keep ships from floundering off the island and to guide ships into the harbor, a lighthouse was erected by Ptolemy II in 270 B.C. The Greek architect Sostratos is given credit for the design, but no sketches of the blueprint have been preserved. Accounts of ancient mariners and scribes disagree as to its height, and vary between estimates of two hundred feet and six hundred feet. All

lighthouses erected after the construction of the Alexandrian lighthouse have been patterned after it. When we passed by Pharos en route to docking at Alexandria in 1979, there was no evidence of any remains of the lighthouse.

Walls of Babylon—The *Encyclopaedia Britannica* co-equals the Walls of Babylon as the Seventh Wonder of the Ancient World. According to descriptions of Babylon recorded in ancient manuscripts, the walls of this magnificent city were three hundred feet high above the ground and thirty-five feet below the ground to keep assaulting armies from either using assault ladders or employing efforts to dig under. The wall was eighty feet thick with two hundred and fifty guard towers and one hundred gates of brass. The wall was fifteen miles on each side, sixty miles in total circumference. The Euphrates River divided the city and provided water for the moats which added extra protection outside the wall, and provided waterways inside the city for transportation. Excavations since 1918 have verified ancient historical accounts. When we were in Babylon in 1978 we were privileged to examine the lower portions of the main Ishtar Gate. The upper portion of the Ishtar Gate was removed by German archaeologists and reassembled in the Pergamon Museum in Berlin.

6. **The Mausoleum at Halicarnassus**–Halicarnassus was the center of a province in southeast Turkey during the time of the Persian Empire. The city was also associated with nearby Kos and Rhodes. Mausolus, the ruler of the province, maintained a closer relationship with Greece than he did with Persia. After the death of

Mausolus, his widow, Artemisia, ruled the province. She erected a temple in her husband's memory. The building was adorned with greenstone, marble, and the work of the best sculptors in Asia. A nine-foot, nine-inch statue of Mausolus stood on a beautiful pedestal surrounded by thirty-six columns. The entire structure was of such artistic excellence and beauty that even today monumental buildings for the dead are called mausoleums. The statue of Mausolus is today in the British Museum in London. Halicarnassus today is the city of Bodrum. I have passed by it on a cruise ship on the way to the island of Rhodes, and also by bus when touring the site of the seven churches of Revelation. Little is left of this Sixth Wonder of the Ancient World.

5. **Temple of Artemis (Diana) at Ephesus**—Artemis was one of the mythological goddesses worshipped by the Greeks. The Roman counterpart was Diana. In mythology, Artemis was the daughter of Zeus (Greek for Satan), and she was also the sister of Apollo. The cult of Diana set aside a week in the spring to honor her as the mother of birth. This holiday was called Ephesia, thus the city of Ephesus was given to the goddess worship of Artemis, or Diana (Acts 19:24–28). The Temple of Diana at Ephesus was made of marble and one of the largest in the world at that time. Earthquakes that partially destroyed the city of Ephesus in the second and third centuries A.D. probably also destroyed the Temple of Diana. The remains of the Church of St. John and the Tomb of St. John, which we have visited several times, now occupy the plot of ground on which this Fifth Wonder of the Ancient World once stood.

4. **Colossus of Rhodes**—Depending upon the historical source, the Colossus of Rhodes was finished after eleven

years of work in about 1200 B.C. The sculptor was Charles of Lindus. Lindus was at the opposite end of the island in relation to where the statue was erected. The "colossus" was a two hundred-foot-high image of the mythological sun god Helios. Mariners wrote that when the sun shone upon the idol it could be seen for one hundred miles out to sea. The Colossus of Rhodes stood for one thousand years, until it collapsed into the sea when an earthquake shook the island in 224 B.C. In traveling by bus between the city of Rhodes and Lindus we noted that a huge earthquake fault paralleled the highway, and tremors still occur quite frequently. Pieces of the statue lay in the water until a trader from the Saracens, a Jew, bought the scrap metal. Some historical notes suggest the legs of the statue stood on either side of the bay entrance to the city, but having entered this harbor several times, we know this would have been impossible. We believe the legs were on either side of a small inlet where several ships could have docked. In A.D. 1300 the last of the Crusaders left the Castle of the Knights in Lebanon and went to Rhodes. Today, Rhodes is part of the Greek island archipelago and serves as a tourist vacation site. No evidence of the once mighty Colossus of Rhodes remains.

3. **Statue of Zeus (Jupiter) at Olympia**—In the early Hellenic periods, Zeus was worshipped as the god of the underworld. Included in the early worship of Zeus were human sacrifices and the eating of human flesh. In later Hellenic times, Zeus became more of a comprehensive deity and the Greeks more civilized, thus, human sacrificial worship ceased. While there were many statues and temples dedicated to Zeus, the one on Mt. Olympia was so huge and involved the work of so many

highly skilled artists that it has been accepted as the third greatest Wonder of the Ancient World. The statue of the king of mythological gods was forty feet high, seated upon a throne. His flesh was made of pure ivory, his robe and ornaments of gold, and the monument was placed in a temple such as only the Greeks could construct. The sculptor was Phidias who completed this, his greatest work, in 457 B.C. There was also a magnificent Temple of Zeus at Pergamos, and we believe Jesus referred to it as "Satan's seat" (Rev. 2:13). We have been to both Pergamos and Olympia. The only evidence left of the Temple of Zeus at Pergamos is the bare floor. At Olympia there are many artifacts on top of the mountain, but there were none that we could identify with Zeus. Probably both the statue and the temple were pillaged by invaders for the ivory, gold, and precious stones.

2. **Hanging Gardens of Babylon**—Babylon was never destroyed as were Sodom and Gomorrah, as prophesied in Isaiah 13 and Jeremiah 51–52. The final destruction of Babylon is yet future. Gradually, after A.D. 100, Babylon was slowly buried under the sands of the Euphrates River. In 1972 the restoration of Babylon by Saddam Hussein began. When we were in Babylon in 1978 we inspected the Hanging Gardens as they appeared from the sand. The so-called Hanging Gardens were brick terraces which appeared to be hanging seventy-five feet above the ground. Recently, Hussein offered a reward for anyone who could offer a reasonable explanation as to how the gardens were watered. In 1987 Iraq held a one-month international festival in Babylon to celebrate the city's restoration. The Hanging Gardens are the only one of the Seven

Wonders of the Ancient World to be restored to even a resemblance of its former state.

1. **The Great Pyramid of Giza**—The greatest of all the Seven Wonders of the Ancient World is the Great Pyramid of Giza, near Cairo, Egypt. We will limit our observations about this mighty monument for the time being, as we will be devoting several chapters in this book to its importance—historically and prophetically.

How and why the roster of the Seven Wonders of the Ancient World are so determined and in which order is not really known to this author. There are worlds of men and nations that occurred before the birth of Christ that are of equal, or even greater significance and amazement than some of the so-called Seven Wonders. To name just a few which I have personally seen:

The Temples of Luxor and Karnak
The Valley of the Kings
Queen Hatshepsut Mausoleum
The Land of the Thousand Mounds in Galatia
Stonehenge in England
The Monoliths of Easter Island
Petra in Jordan
The Great Wall of China
The Terra Cotta Army of Sion

We would also think that the Temple on Mt. Moriah would at least deserve consideration as being one of the wonders of the ancient world, but we know by the Word of God that nothing that man does is beyond the permissive will of the Creator. We know by the example of the Tower of Babel that without the restraining influence of God, man can build anything that he can imagine. Therefore, who imagined to build the Great Pyramid, and why did God allow the building of this mighty wonder in the land of Egypt? This is the subject which we will next consider in the light of God's Word and His eternal plan and purpose.

The Pyramid of Khafre, thought to be the son of Cheops, adjacent to the Great Pyramid of Giza. Original limestone casing blocks are still in evidence at the top. Consensus places construction at 2600 B.C.

Magnificent mausoleum of Queen Hatshepsut of the eighteenth dynasty, 1500 B.C., at Luxor. She was co-ruler with Tuthmosis III, who hated her so much he deleted her face and name from all records. Architech was the queen's lover.

Cheops' ship, preserved in a large vault by the Great Pyramid. Although almost fifty centuries old, wood and rope and rigging were in excellent condition. Workmanship rivals any today.

Above is a gold funeral mask that covered the head and face of Tutankhamen. The mask, made in his likeness, indicated he was quite young when he died.

Most of the tombs and buildings that have survived the earthquakes and pillaging are decorated with sculpture and art in beautiful colors which remain true after thousands of years.

The author, Noah Hutchings, mounting a camel for a ride to the pyramids at Giza. Camels remain a valuable beast of burden in desert regions of the Middle East and North Africa.

Inner coffin that held the sarcophagus of Tutankhamen, pharaoh of the eighteenth dynasty, 1350 B.C. It is of exquisite workmanship, overlaid with gold and ivory, and placed inside a wooden coffin.

The Great Pyramid of Cheops which remained closed until the ninth century. Consensus places construction at 2650 B.C. Limestone casing blocks were removed by the Turks for building purposes. Notice the missing headstone.

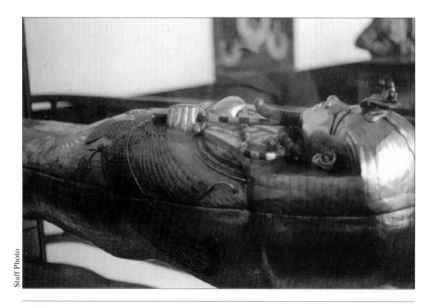

Sarcophagus of Tutankhamen taken from his tomb, Valley of the Kings, at Luxor in 1922, the date of discovery—one of the very few that had not already been opened and robbed for treasure.

The imagination is taxed to visualize the art and labor that went into the construction of the ancient Egyptian temples like the ones at Luxor.

Remains of temples and tombs at Luxor on the edge of the desert near Karnak. Scaffolding was composed of a temporary wall of huge bricks made with straw; some still remain, indicating Hebrew slaves could have helped with construction.

Remains of Luxor Temple. Notice the height of the statue in contrast to nearby tourists. Also notice the size of the pillars which supported a limestone roof once decorated with the star map of the heavens.

Staff Photo

One of the several gates to Karnak Temple, three miles south of Luxor. Karnak is approximately one square mile, filled with the remains of temples to commemorate reigns of various kings and queens. Huge obelisks engraved with chronicles and religious beliefs still stand.

Staff Photo

Giant sentinels of Thebes guarding the road to Queen Hatshepsut's mausoleum and the Valley of the Kings which lies just on the other side of the mountain seen in the background.

One of the smaller statues of Ramses II, nineteenth dynasty, 1300 B.C., at Memphis. Memphis was the capitol of Egypt for one thousand years, and some of the statues of Ramses II were almost one hundred feet in height.

Main gate at Karnak. Karnak and Luxor were united by a large three-mile avenue lined with thousands of huge rams carved out of stone. Again, the work and artisanship staggers the imagination.

A lone obelisk still stands guard over the ruins of a Karnak temple dedicated to an ancient pharaoh.

Chapter Two

The Pillar of Enoch

Almost due west of Cairo, Egypt, just across the Nile River, stands the only remaining one of the ancient Seven Wonders of the World—the Great Pyramid. This particular pyramid covers an area of thirteen acres and was originally some four hundred and eighty-five feet in height. There are approximately 2.5 million stone building blocks remaining, even though the outside casing stones have been removed. The blocks weigh from three to thirty tons each. Napoleon, when he viewed this edifice, estimated that he could build a wall ten feet high all the way around France with its stones. If the stones were cut into one-foot sections, there would be enough to reach all the way around the equator. All of the locomotives in the world together could not move them, and there is enough room within the pyramid to contain all the cathedrals in Rome, Milan, and Florence, with space left over for the Empire State Building, Westminster Abbey, St. Paul's Cathedral, and the Houses of Parliament.

The Great Pyramid was probably standing in Egypt when Abraham planted his feet on the banks of the Nile, and it was most certainly there when Moses led the children of Israel through the Red Sea. It would indeed be strange if this greatest edifice on the face of the Earth were not mentioned in the Bible. We believe that it is noted in several scriptures, two of which we will make mention of at this time.

In that day shall there be an altar to the LORD in the midst of the land of Egypt, and a pillar at the border thereof to the LORD. And it shall be for a sign and for a witness unto the LORD of hosts in the land of Egypt: for they shall cry unto the LORD because of the oppressors, and he shall send them a saviour, and a great one, and he shall deliver them. And the LORD shall be known to Egypt, and the Egyptians shall know the LORD in that day . . . (Isa. 19:19–21).

And we read in verse 22: "And the LORD shall smite Egypt: he shall smite and heal it." The setting for this scripture is, of course, the Day of the Lord. The smiting of Egypt refers to a great judgment that will come upon that nation as a result of its part in the conspiracy to destroy Israel. We read in Ezekiel 29:9–13:

And the land of Egypt shall be desolate and waste; and they shall know that I am the LORD: because he hath said, The river [Nile] is mine, and I have made it. Behold, therefore I am against thee, and against thy rivers, and I will make the land of Egypt utterly waste and desolate, from the tower of Syene even unto the border of Ethiopia. No foot of man shall pass through it, nor foot of beast shall pass through it, neither shall it be inhabited forty years. And I will make the land of Egypt desolate in the midst of the countries that are desolate, and her cities among the cities that are laid waste shall be desolate forty years: and I will scatter the Egyptians among the nations, and will disperse them through the countries. Yet thus saith the Lord GOD; At the end of forty years will I gather the Egyptians from the people whither they were scattered.

Thus, we see the smiting and the subsequent healing of Egypt when the Lord comes, as prophesied by both Isaiah and Ezekiel. This judgment may be in the form of atomic contamination inasmuch as the land will be poisoned at the surface for forty years. Not even a dog will be able to pass over the ground without suffering death.

However, according to Isaiah, the altar to the Lord that stands in the midst of the land of Egypt, and at the border, will be an important sign to the Egyptians in the days of the healing of their land that the Lord God of Israel is the true God.

During the first dynasty Egypt was divided into two king-doms. Because of its great antiquity, no one knows the exact date the first Egyptian dynasty began. The twelfth dynasty was already established, according to the Egyptian historian Manetho, in 2000 B.C., at the time of Abraham. Some place the first dynasty as far back as 4000 B.C., long before the flood. How-ever, according to Dr. Zaki Y. Saad, noted scholar of Egyptian history, the first dynasty began in about 3200 B.C. King Aha of the first dynasty ruled over Upper Egypt, and Queen Neithetep ruled over Lower Egypt. The two monarchs united their king-doms into one empire through matrimony, and the boundary of the resulting kingdom was about the same as that of modern Egypt today. The Great Pyramid stands on the old border that divided Lower Egypt from Upper Egypt, in the geographic cen-ter of the united kingdom. Therefore, the Great Pyramid alone fits the description given by Isaiah of "an altar to the LORD in the midst of the land," yet "a pillar at the border." And, inas-much as Isaiah said that the Great Pyramid would be known as a sign unto the Lord (evidently looking forward to a day when its secrets would be unlocked), it must indeed be in reality a Bible in stone.

We read also in Jeremiah 32:17,20:

Ah Lord GOD! behold, thou hast made the heaven and the earth by thy great power and stretched out arm, and there is nothing too hard for thee . . . Which hast set signs and wonders in the land of Egypt, even unto this day. . . .

Let us keep in mind that the Great Pyramid is one of the Seven

Wonders of the Ancient World, and possibly the greatest wonder of all ages. According to an article on the Great Pyramid that appeared in the June 1972, edition of *Saga* magazine, no construction company in the world today could erect such a building. Quoting from *Halley's Bible Handbook:*

> The amazing thing about the pyramids is that they were built at the dawn of history. Sir Flinders Petrie calls the Pyramid of Cheops "the greatest and most accurate structure the world has ever seen." The *Encyclopaedia Britannica* says, "The brain power to which it testifies is as great as that of any modern man."

The degree of engineering, mathematical, and astronomical skill and knowledge that was required to build this mighty monument shall be discussed in more detail later. For the present however, try to imagine constructing a building the size of the Great Pyramid with stone blocks weighing up to thirty tons each, and then having the building stand for at least four thousand years without its foundation settling so much as a fraction of an inch! When we consider this, we begin to get some measure of appreciation for its scientific perfection.

The latest date mentioned for the completion of the Great Pyramid is 2170 B.C., a date proposed by Dr. John Herschel because of the fact that in that year a line drawn from the center of the pyramid base through its apex would intersect the star Alcyone in the heavens. Also, as of that year, the long, straight shaft up the subterranean chamber would have pointed exactly to Alpha Draconis, the polar star of that year. This position of these two stars in the sky in relation to the Great Pyramid will not occur again until the completion of the precession of the equinoxes, or 25,857 years later. It is also amazing to note that when the length of the diagonals of the pyramid's base (in pyramid inches) is totaled, we have exactly 25,857 inches. The only thing wrong with Dr. Herschel's theory is that the builders of the pyramid could not possibly have known beforehand that it would be completed on a certain date.

As indicated in *The Great Pyramid: Proof of God*, by George R. Riffert, measurements and mathematical equations within the Great Pyramid indicate that within the divine cubit, or royal cubit, the English inch is .001 too short. It requires 10,011 English inches to equal 10,000 pyramid inches. The importance of this difference, even though minute, will be referred to later in this book.

There are some who date the building of the pyramid from 4000 B.C., which would be about the time that Adam was created. There are scriptures which we shall discuss later that indicate this possibility, but most historians and archaeologists believe that it was built during the reign of the Egyptian king Cheops. Dr. Leonard Cottrell, in his excellent book, *Lost Pharaohs*, offers considerable evidence to substantiate his belief that it was built for Cheops. We have no great objection to this thesis because no one really knows just who Cheops was and when he lived. The dictionary places Cheops at 2900 B.C., or before the flood in the time of the biblical figure Enoch. Who is to say that Cheops was not Enoch himself? Ancient records show that Noah had at least one hundred names, depending upon where the account of the flood was recorded. Nimrod also had many names.

Dr. Cottrell says of the origin of the pyramids: "Beginning a chapter on the pyramids is like being asked to describe a sunset, or the arrival of spring." Even those who have studied ancient Egyptian culture and the pyramids for years are often reluctant to establish hard and fast dates, or to identify the builders.

Herodotus, the Greek historian who came to Egypt in 450 B.C., interviewed the Egyptian priests and was informed that the ancient King Cheops built the Great Pyramid. He supposedly used one hundred thousand men at a time, working in three-month shifts. The construction was said to have taken thirty years, but we must remember that Herodotus' account was relayed from traditions that had been handed down for twenty-five hundred years. Manetho gave a different version. He wrote: "There came up from the east, men of ignoble race, who had the confidences to invade our country, and easily subdued it by their power, without a battle." According to Manetho, these men built the pyramids. It is possible they were subjects of the shepherd kings of Abraham's day. So hated were they by the Egyptians that they refused to mention their name. According to Genesis 46:34, even when Joseph was in Egypt hundreds of years later, "every shepherd is an abomination unto the Egyptians." Other traditions name Melchizedek as the builder of the Great Pyramid, but perhaps the most interesting of all the accounts given is the one by J. Bernard Nicklin in his book, *Testimony in Stone:*

> The late David Davidson . . . drew attention to the remarkable way the age, or dynasty, of Enoch is impressed upon the Great Pyramid itself. As Enoch lived 365 years (Gen. 5:23), so 365, or to be more exact, 365.242 days, the value of the solar year, forms the basis of all its measurements. Moreover, by ancient writers, the Great Pyramid is described as "the Pillar of Enoch." Enoch was in the line of Seth, and Josephus ascribes the building of it to the dynasty of Seth. So that Enoch—the year-circle man—who, it should be observed, is referred to as a prophet (Jude 14–15), may well have been the architect, if not the builder, of the Great Pyramid. Now, if God revealed the plan of the tabernacle to Moses, and gave instructions for building the temple to David, could He not also have revealed the design and measurements of the Great Pyramid to the one chosen by Him to superintend its erection? In fact, could He not have inspired and guided all concerned in the task?

Before we disregard the suggestion that Enoch may have been

the builder of the Great Pyramid, let us keep in mind that the most common date given for the beginning of the construction of the Pyramid of Cheops is about 2900 B.C., or right before the period during which Enoch lived.

Although it required superhuman knowledge and skill to build the Great Pyramid, the reason for its construction and that of all the pyramids and tombs of Egypt, was so that man might inherit eternal life, or so they believed. The earliest beliefs of the Egyptians, whether we call them Egyptians or antediluvians, were quite in accord with basic Christian doctrine. We quote Dr. Zaki Y. Saad from his book, *The Excavations at Helwan:*

> In these tombs we were astonished to find the doors placed in the southwest section of the ceilings in the burial chambers. In each tomb the stela was . . . positioned to face the body inside the chamber. Our conclusion was that Egyptians of the Second Dynasty believed that the soul of the dead departed to heaven at the moment of death and that later, when the soul descended . . . it would . . . identify its original body. Thus it appears that only later did the Egyptians come to a belief that the soul remained in the tomb with the body.

Dr. Saad also relates that the remains of the ancients who died in Egypt during the first and second dynasties, long before the flood, were buried in the ground in the same position as a baby in the mother's womb. The bones have not decayed because the region has been dry for thousands of years. They were buried in this fashion because those who had faith in a resurrection believed that they would have to be born again. The position indicated a faith in the coming of a new body, a·body that would never die.

Josephus believed the Great Pyramid was built before the

flood by the sons of Seth, of whom Enoch was a member:

> Now this Seth, when he was brought up, and came to those years which he could discern what was good, became a man; and as he was himself of an excellent character, so did he leave children behind him who imitated his virtues. All these proved to be of good disposition. They also inhabited the same country without dissension, and in a happy condition, without any misfortunes falling upon them, till they died. They also were the inventors of the peculiar sort of wisdom which is concerned with the heavenly bodies, and their order. And that their inventions might not be lost before they were sufficiently known, upon Adam's prediction that the world was to be destroyed at one time by the force of fire, and at another time by the violence and quantity of water, they made two pillars; the one of brick, the other of stone: they inscribed their discoveries on them both, that in case the pillar of brick should be destroyed by the flood, the pillar of stone might remain, and exhibit those discoveries to mankind, and also inform them that there was another pillar of brick erected by them. Now this remains in the land of Siriad to this day.

In the time of Josephus the land of Siriad was a part of Egypt in which the false religion of Sirius was practiced, and there can be little doubt that Josephus was referring to the Great Pyramid, since it reflects astronomical knowledge beyond even that of today. This knowledge, according to Josephus, was known to the descendants of Seth, and was incorporated into the building of this great monument in Egypt.

Josephus was a priest of Israel who became governor of the province of Galilee. His Jewish name was Joseph. He began the great rebellion against the Romans in A.D. 66. He was captured by Vespasian and spent two years in the camp of Vespasian's son, Captain Titus, watching the siege and final destruction of Jerusalem and the Temple. The Romans gave Josephus all the writings of the scribes and the prophets that were in the Temple and Jerusalem to write a history of Israel so that the world might know there was such a nation. It is doubtful if Josephus would have written anything in his books, *Wars of the Jews* and *Antiquities of the Jews*, plus his *Dissertations*, that could not have been supported or documented by written evidence, physical evidence, or common knowledge or traditions. Also, as we read of the consensus by contemporary historians on the cover of *Josephus*, translated by William Whiston:

> Scholars of more recent days say of Josephus that ". . . he had the most essential qualifications for a historian—a perfect accurate knowledge of all of the transactions which he relates, without prejudices to mislead him in the representation of them. . . ."

It should be noted that in *Antiquities*, chapter 18, Josephus injected his own personal testimony that Jesus was the Christ.

As we would expect, Josephus wrote in Hebrew. The texts in Hebrew were later translated into Greek, and from the Greek into many other languages. It is in *Antiquities of the Jews*, chapter 3, where Josephus wrote about the sons of Seth building a pillar of brick and a pillar of stone wherein was incorporated knowledge to the heavens and Earth. William Whiston, who translated Josephus from the Greek to English, footnoted this chapter with his own reference that although this information doubtless referred to the Great Pyramid in Siriad, or the Cairo area, Josephus must be in error because no structure could have survived the great geological upheavals of the flood. But we should keep in mind the tremendous weight of the Great Pyramid, that it was erected on a solid rock foundation and sealed with one hundred and forty-four thousand limestone blocks. In addition, if it was built by the will of God, it would have survived regardless of the catastrophe. And even more weight is added to this account by Josephus in that this was not merely his own opinion, but the conclusions and writings of scribes and prophets (including Jeremiah and Isaiah), as well as peers and contemporaries.

The *Encyclopaedia Britannica* places Cheops, the Egyptian pharaoh credited with the building of the Great Pyramid, between either 3969–3908 B.C., a lifespan of sixty years, or 2900–2839 B.C. The latter figure is the most accepted. Also, several ancient historians, including Herodotus and Manetho, are referenced. Herodotus seems to have gotten confused about which Egyptian kings lived in which dynasties and, therefore, his information is mostly discounted. Manetho seems to have been more accurate, but from the combined historical notes it would seem that Cheops closed the temples and stopped sacrifices to the gods resulting in a religious revolution and rebellion. Outside the Great Pyramid, only two or three artifacts can be traced to his reign. One ambiguous historical source noted recently on a television documentary about the Great Pyramid that Cheops went to visit an island in the Nile River. He never returned and there is little or no information about what may have happened to him. It is certain that his body was not placed within the coffer in the Great Pyramid. We are again placed with the possibility presented by Clarence Larkin, Dr. J. A. Seiss, and others that this same Cheops could have been Enoch.

Enoch is our spiritual father, or predecessor, in the heavenly translation. We read in Hebrews 11:5: "By faith Enoch was translated that he should not see death; and was not found, because God had translated him: for before his translation he had this testimony, that he pleased God."

The lesser pyramids, which were all patterned after the Great Pyramid, were built as vehicles of heavenly translation for the kings under whose reign they were constructed. The king's body was placed in a coffin within a specially-built room inside the pyramid where it would await transportation into the next world. It is amazing that no body was found in the Throne Room of the Great Pyramid. This recalls the statement concerning the life of Enoch in Genesis 5:24: "And Enoch walked with God: and he was not; for God took him." If Enoch was in fact the builder of the Great Pyramid, it would explain why the king's body is missing, while all the other pyramids contained bodies.

Let us keep in mind whether it is revealed in the heavens, etched in monuments of stone, or recorded in the Bible, that the truth of God is pressed upon the human mind to bring the individual to the reality of John 3:3,16: "Verily, verily, I say unto thee, Except a man be born again, he cannot see the kingdom of God. . . . For God so loved the world, that he gave his only begotten Son, that whosoever believeth in him should not perish, but have everlasting life."

Chapter Three

Mathematical Mysteries
of the Great Pyramid

When God gave Moses the blueprint for the Tabernacle, which was an earthly pattern of the Temple in Heaven, He dictated the exact measurements. We read in Isaiah 40:12 that even the dust of the Earth is measured.

We are living, we believe, in that generation spoken of in Daniel 12:4: "But thou, O Daniel, shut up the words, and seal the book, even to the time of the end: many shall run to and fro, and knowledge shall be increased."

It has been claimed that today knowledge is doubling every two and one-half years. In times past there have been periods in which knowledge has increased in certain areas of human intelligence: music, literature, agriculture, metallurgy, aerodynamics, astronomy, electronics, nuclear physics, geology, mechanics, plastics, communications. At the base of the knowledge explosion in these latter years is man's development and application of the science of mathematics and, in particular, computer science. A computer is a mathematical machine developed to the degree that it can apply the laws of mathematical science to any given problem and situation. Without the computer, modern space exploration would not have been possible.

The word "mathematics" comes from the Greek, *mathematikos,* or the Latin, *mathematicus,* and means "to learn," "inclined to learn," or "memory." A computer is a sophisticated mathematical machine, but it is only as useful as its memory. If a computer loses its memory, it is of no use. It is the ultimate projection and application of the meaning of the word "mathematics" coined by the Greeks almost three thousand years ago.

However, God is the Master Mathematician of the universe. He is the author of all science, and by His laws of creation all things consist. The base of all absolute mathematics is the fact that one plus one equals two. From the beginning, in Genesis 1:3, we read on the first day of creation that God spoke, "and there was light." On the next day of creation, God spoke and the firmament, or our atmosphere, appeared. We read in Genesis 1:8: "And God called the firmament Heaven. And the evening and the morning were the second day." The first chapter of Genesis plainly informs us that one plus one equals two. On the next day, God made the dry land and plant life appear, and here we are told that two plus one equals three. In Genesis we discover division. God divided Adam into two parts, and from one came two. We are also told that man, through procreation, multiplied upon the face of the Earth.

Through the chronology of mankind in Genesis we see the development of the numerical system to nearly one thousand, i.e., Methuselah lived to be 969 years of age before he died. Then, from the beginning of simple arithmetic in Genesis, we discover progressively the development of mathematics until we get to Revelation, where there is revealed a complicated system of numerics involving patterns of sevens, tens, and other numbers. In Revelation 9:16 we find the number, "two hundred thousand thousand" (200,000,000).

The mathematical structure of our Bible proves beyond doubt that it was written by a Master Mathematician. He is the same Creator who established wonders in the land of Egypt.

Let us consider the mathematical and logistical problems

that the builders of the Great Pyramid had to confront almost five thousand years ago when there were no computers, railroads, or self-propelled hydraulic cranes.

Let us assume there are slaves to hack out 2,600,000 giant blocks from the quarries. What kind of tools did they use to carve out the stone? There was no dynamite, no explosive, in those days. Where did they get the tools? After the blocks were quarried, how were they dressed? Some of those stones were fitted with seamless joints. Dressing . . . would require a minimum pressure of two tons! Where does a primitive workman get the equipment to apply that pressure? Third, how do you get the stones to the building site at Giza? Fourth, how could a small country like Egypt feed all those slaves? Fifth, where did they get the ropes to pull those blocks? In ancient Egypt, you didn't dash into town to buy rope. How much rope would you need to handle 2,600,000 stone blocks? These stones weigh a minimum of three tons. Let's assume we need four times as many ropes as stones. Some of the ropes could be used again, so we'd need about two times as many ropes as stones. That's an incredible 5 million pieces of rope—good sturdy rope. Where did they get it? Sixth, where did the Pharaoh find an architect who could design a building with such precise measurements? . . . At the completion rate of ten stones a day, it would have taken 260,000 days to build the pyramid. That is 712 years! Modern builders are pleased when they obtain an accuracy of one-tenth of an inch on their construction projects. Yet, the pyramid is built with far greater precision, despite being honeycombed with tunnels, shafts, and bizarre hidden chambers. . . . Find me a construction company that will guarantee to build a 6.5 million-ton building without settling. It can't be done. There are endless mysteries on how the pyramids were constructed. An example is the remarkable "king's" chamber deep inside the structure with two rows of 70-ton blocks of rare, red granite formed into a unique roof. These stones could only have been taken from quarries that are 600 miles from Giza. The horse and cart were not brought to Egypt until the 17th Dynasty. How did they transport these stones over such an enormous distance? Historians say the 70-ton blocks, and smaller stones, were pushed overland on wooden rollers. Trees were chopped down, dressed out to logs, and used as rollers under the blocks. It's a good theory except for the trees. There are no forests in Egypt. There would have been a loss factor of about 10 rollers per stone. The Great Pyramid would have required 26 million wooden rollers. . . . The theory of primitive people building the pyramid with their hands simply doesn't stand inspection. (*Saga*, June 1972, "The Fantastic Mystery of the Pyramids")

George R. Riffert in his book, *Great Pyramid: Proof of God*, says:

This amazing work in stone honors Egypt, but adds no glory to the civilization native to that land; for while it stands in Egypt, it is not of Egypt. The pyramid is intensely religious in symbolism, purpose, and themes, but carries no religious marks or signs of any kind. And standing as it does, in the most idolatrous country of the world, where practically every living or creeping thing was worshipped, and where the emblems of religion were on everything from jewelry and household articles to temples and tombs, the total absence of such marks from the pyramids is most significant.

The conclusion reached by the two previous references should add credibility to the statement by Josephus that the Great Pyramid antedated the flood by Divine design and power.

The July 14, 1969, edition of the *London Times* carried the following report:

Scientists who have been trying to x-ray the pyramid at Giza, near Cairo, are baffled by mysterious influences that are throwing into utter confusion the reading of their space age electronic equipment.

For 24 hours a day for more than a year, in the hopes of finding secret chambers thought to exist within the 6 million-ton mass of the pyramid, they have been recording on magnetic tape the pattern of cosmic rays reaching the interior. The idea is that as the rays strike the pyramid uniformly from all directions , they should, if the pyramid is solid, be recorded uniformly by a detector in the chamber at the bottom. But if there were vaults above the detector, they would let more rays through than the solid areas, thereby revealing their existence. More than $1 million and thousands of man-hours have been spent on the project which was expected to reach a climax a few months ago when the latest IBM 1120 computer was delivered to Ein Shams University, near Cairo. At Ein Shams, Dr. Amr. Gohed, in charge of the installation at the pyramid, showed me the new IBM 1120 computer surrounded by hundreds of tins of recordings from the pyramid, stacked up in date order. Though hesitant at first, he told me of the impasse that had been reached. It defies all the known laws of science and electronics, he said, picking up a tin of recordings. He put the tape through the computer, which traced the pattern of cosmic ray particles on paper. He then selected a recording made the next day and put it through the computer. But the recording was completely different. "This is scientifically impossible," he told me. After a long discussion, I asked Dr. Gohed, "Has this scientific know-how been rendered useless by some force beyond man's comprehension?" He hesitated before replying, then said: "Either the geometry of the pyramid is in substantial error, which would affect our readings, or there is a mystery which is beyond explanation—call it what you will, occultism, the curse of the pharaohs, sorcery, or magic—there is some force that defies the laws of science at work in the pyramids!"

Dr. Luis Alvarez, winner of the 1968 Nobel Prize for physics, developed the method of measuring cosmic rays streaming through the pyramids, and so we can see the superior scientific knowledge that went into their construction not only cannot be duplicated, but cannot even be *deciphered*. Dr. Gunther Rosenbery said of these scientific experiments, "Even with our marvelous computers, man can't solve the enigma of the pyramids."

The Great Pyramid is mathematically perfect in its location, which is, according to Isaiah 19:19-20, in the middle of Egypt and on the border between the old kingdoms of Upper and Lower Egypt. In 1968, Professor H. Mitchell of the United States Survey Service was sent to report on the construction of the Suez Canal. While studying maps of the coastal regions of Egypt, he was intrigued by the curvature of the shoreline of the Nile delta. He drew a curved line through all the prominent locations along the coast and found that the line formed an arc whose center was located at the site of the Great Pyramid.

The Great Pyramid was constructed on solid rock that was leveled around the base lines, with cornerstones which were sunk eight inches into the rock. Measurements were made in the Hebrew cubit, which is 25.025 inches in length. The length of each base line is 365.2422 cubits, the exact number of days in the solar year. Our calendar is 365 days, but an extra day is added every fourth year in the month of February to allow for the fractional day. The angle of slope of the sides of the pyramid is such that they meet at an apex with a predetermined height of 232.52 cubits. Why did the designer make it exactly this height?

When twice the length of the base is divided by this number, we get the number 3.14159, or *pi*, the relationship of the diameter of a circle to its circumference. The Greeks were given credit for this discovery, but it is evident that it was known by the designer of the Great Pyramid at least twenty-five hundred years prior to Greek geometry.

The perimeter of the base of the pyramid is equal to the circumference of a circle whose diameter is twice the height of the pyramid, and thus we see in the equality of these figures the solution to the difficult problem of how to square the circle. For every ten feet up the slope of the pyramid, one rises nine feet in altitude, and by multiplying the altitude of the pyramid by ten raised to the ninth power, one arrives at the figure 91,840,000, which is the distance of the Earth from the sun in miles.

Each heavenly body has its own peculiar year, and as we have already pointed out, Earth's year is given in the mathematical design of the Great Pyramid. The difference in the position of the stars in the heavens in relation to Earth differs by about fifty seconds of arc each year, and for the stars to complete a cycle and return to the exact position where they were at any one period of time requires a time period of 25,827 years. When the diagonals of the pyramid's base, in pyramid inches, are added together, the sum total is exactly 25,827 inches. It is astounding to think that such knowledge was possible five thousand years before the birth of the space age and all its complex computers. Surely a wisdom greater than man's must have designed and supervised the construction of the Great Pyramid.

According to George Riffert, author of the book, *Great Pyramid: Proof of God*, the pyramid stands in the exact center of the land mass of the world. Furthermore, by multiplying its total weight by 1,000 trillion, we arrive at a figure equal to the weight of the Earth. The cornerstones at the four base points determine true east, west, north, and south on the compass, so that when the sun crosses the equinox no shadow is cast anywhere on all four sides. The mean ocean and land level of Earth is 455 feet above the Great Pyramid's baseline, and it is at this exact height where the top course of masonry ends. Who could have made such a precise geodetic survey of the world and incorporated this data in the design of this structure? Or for that matter, who could have surveyed the heavens, for the angle of the descending passage indicates that it is pointing to the center of the universe, around which all other galaxies are rotating.

For thousands of years men thought that the Earth was flat, or that all other heavenly bodies revolved around the Earth. But the designer of the Great Pyramid evidently knew this was not the case: he knew that the Earth revolved around the sun; that all planets, stars, and galaxies were traversing a circular path; and the entire mass was revolving in a greater circle around some common focal point. We again come to the only possible answer—that God must have either designed it or revealed this wisdom to the builders as suggested by Psalm 19:4-6:

> Their line is gone out through all the earth, and their words to the end of the world. In them hath he set a tabernacle for the sun, Which is as a bridegroom coming out of his chamber, and rejoiceth as a strong man to run a race. His going forth is from the end of the heaven, and his circuit unto the ends of it: and there is nothing hid from the heat thereof.

Each side of the Great Pyramid, measured from corner sockets, is 9,140 British inches. Piazzi Smyth, perhaps the first to intensively study the Great Pyramid, was puzzled as to why the baseline of each of the sides were curved inwardly at the exact middle to a depth of three feet. Upon further investigation he discovered that in relation to the entire pyramid, the curve corresponded to the exact curvature of the Earth. For thousands of years after the flood, the best minds thought the Earth was flat. And, if you stand off and survey the Great Pyramid at a distance, each side looks straight, or flat. Yet, for perfect construction, both visual and physical, the sides needed to be curved to match the degree of the curvature of the Earth.

The Greeks, over two thousand years after the construction of the Great Pyramid, built another near perfect structure, the Parthenon. The sides and the pillars in the Parthenon were likewise curved inwardly, matching the curvature of the sides of the

Great Pyramid. The Parthenon, although suffering some internal refurbishing from a temple, to a church, to a mosque, stood as a near perfect construction example without even the smallest crack for over two thousand years. In 1687, when the Parthenon was used by the Turks as an ammunition arsenal, a tremendous explosion blew off part of the roof and shattered many of the beautiful pillars. But even today, the Parthenon still stands as an example of artistic and enduring construction. The Greeks are given the credit for geometric theorems and postulates which undergird contemporary mathematics. However, the Greeks simply used mathematical and construction principles that were used even before the flood.

Piazzi Smyth, on pages 41–42 of his book, *The Great Pyramid*, observed:

> Modern Egyptologists and the ancient Egyptians, and all the rest of the pagan world too, both see, and saw, nothing in it. . . . Greek mythologists and idolaters through the years were, by merely dividing the pyramid's base-side length by the number of days in a year . . . acquired to themselves, with both ease and accuracy, the most valuable scientific standard of length contained in the whole physical earth. . . . Christians have now no need to bow to anything Grecian, for learning either the laws of the Heavens or the facts of the Great Pyramid.

Larry Pahl, in his book, *The Great Pyramid: The Ancient Mystery Unraveled*, copyrighted 1996, observed:

> Many architects and engineers who have studied the Pyramid's structure contend that, with all our vaunted technological prowess, we could not build the structure today. Does the theory of evolution work in reverse?

There is an Arab proverb which states: "Man fears time, yet time fears the pyramids." Only in the twentieth century when knowledge has increased according to Daniel's prophecy, has the Great Pyramid come to be recognized as a fulfillment of Isaiah's prophecy that in the middle of Egypt, yet on the border, there would be an altar to the Lord. The Great Pyramid still stands in Giza— *Gizeh* means "border." It was built when Egypt was still divided at where the Great Pyramid stands today.

Considering all the known data about the Great Pyramid, it indeed qualifies as the foundational stone of the Earth, and we believe that this particular monument was what God had in mind when He spoke to the suffering Job:

> Where wast thou when I laid the foundations of the earth? declare, if thou hast understanding. Who hath laid the measures thereof, if thou knowest? or who hath stretched the line upon it? Whereupon are the foundations thereof fastened? or who laid the corner stone thereof; When the morning stars sang together, and all the sons of God shouted for joy? (Job 38:4-7).

Chapter Four

The Great Pyramid and Immortality

Man was created with the contingency of death hanging over his head. We read in Genesis 2:15–17:

> And the LORD God took the man, and put him into the garden of Eden to dress it and to keep it. And the LORD God commanded the man, saying, Of every tree of the garden thou mayest freely eat: But of the tree of the knowledge of good and evil, thou shalt not eat of it: for in the day that thou eatest thereof thou shalt surely die.

The sin of the first man and the first woman against the commandment of God brought the sentence of death upon the human race, as we read in the solemn and dread words of the Creator in Genesis 3:19:

> In the sweat of thy face shalt thou eat bread, till thou return unto the ground; for out of it wast thou taken: for dust thou art, and unto dust shalt thou return.

I have been to Ur where there is the ornate tomb of an ancient queen, buried with her chariot, jewels, and servants—things she could use in the afterlife. I have been to the Valley of the Kings and seen the magnificent tombs of the pharaohs, with their entire life set forth in the long galleyway leading to the coffer. There is usually a band of cobras from the door to the coffer (in some tombs the distance may be several hundred feet). If the cobras are pointed toward the coffer, this meant the king was an evil king. If pointed outward, the king was a good ruler. In symbols and hieroglyphics, the life and accomplishments of the king are recorded, along with the Egyptian gods he served. Then, in colored graphics, the king's heart is weighed in a balance. On the other end of the scales is a feather. If the king's heart is heavier than the feather, he is turned over to the god of the underworld. If the feather is heavier than the pharaoh's heart, then he will live forever with the gods of heaven. Every temple, tomb, and pyramid in Egypt manifested an effort to obtain eternal life through works. The Egyptians went the way of the world, the way of Cain.

There is no evidence of any people who feared death more than the ancient Egyptians, and no other people in the history of mankind manifested more hope in a resurrection. Dr. Zaki Y. Saad, in describing the excavations at Helwan, said:

There is no doubt that the Egyptians of the First Dynasty were highly civilized and far advanced in comparison with the other peoples of the period. The buildings discovered in the excavations at Helwan are evidence of the degree of excellence they had achieved in architecture by that remote period. To the ancient Egyptian, his tomb was to be his abode in the other world until the day of resurrection. The Egyptian believed that the other-world life was the real and eternal life and that it was his duty to prepare himself for it by every means. Any negligence in this duty was considered heresy, a falling away from faith in the long and happy life to come, with which one's first life on earth could not compare. Since his other-world abode was so important to his future life, every Egyptian built a tomb that befit his rank and social standing. A man of position and wealth built a tomb as large and pretentious as his means allowed. The interior of his tomb consisted of numerous chambers stored with various objects for him to use and enjoy during his life in the other world.

One visitor to ancient Egypt described it as a "land of the dead" because it was filled with tombs, and the people were eager to sacrifice their material substance in this life in order to lay up treasures for the life to come, a life they believed would never end. Everyone was busy preparing for death, and even the poor, who could afford no tomb, built underground cellars and stocked them with what meager articles they could. It is a mystery where these early inhabitants of the land of Egypt developed such an obsession with death and the afterlife. The first dynasty, according to archaeology, dates back to 3200 B.C., placing these people in the Antediluvian Age.

There is a section of Cairo that I have passed by several times called the City of the Dead. Our guides have told us that the City of the Dead covers an area of one hundred square miles, which would be bigger than most average sized cities in the United States. This is a city of tombs, some as big as ten room houses. The larger tombs were probably for entire families. Today, people with leprosy live in some of the tombs even as they did in the time of Jesus.

I have also been to the Ming tombs and the Ching tombs, the tombs of Lenin and Mao Tse Tung, Flanders Field, Arlington National Cemetery, on the Mt. of Olives where graves and tombs reach all the way to the Eastern Gate, burial vaults in St. Paul's Cathedral in London, plus tombs and cemeteries over much of the world. Animals, birds, or fish do not honor their dead with burial sites: they just walk, or fly off, and leave them. Only man pays honor and respect for the bodies of the dead. Why? Because inwardly, mentally and spiritually, man believes in the resurrection of the dead, regardless whether a person may acknowledge the existence of God or not. As Abraham indicated, many of these people lived beyond, or on the other side of the river, meaning the great flood.

Cities built before the flood have been unearthed by the spade of the archaeologist, and we are informed that mankind multiplied and spread over the face of the Earth prior to the deluge. It also appears that there were different races before the flood, or else the three sons of Noah would not have had different skin pigmentations, as their names indicate. Scholars accept as biblical fact that descendants of Ham resettled the Nile basin in northern Africa, and thereafter returned to the apostasy that infested the antediluvians. The rampant sexual perversion of the pre-flood era was passed on to Ham's son, Canaan, and later bloomed among the Canaanites at Sodom and Gomorrah. Therefore, it is logical to conclude that other forms of apostasy that brought about sexual perversion were also passed on through other descendants of Ham. Let us note carefully the allusion to this apostasy by Paul:

> Because that, when they knew God, they glorified him not as God, neither were thankful; but became vain in their imaginations, and their foolish heart was darkened. Professing themselves to be wise, they became fools, And changed the glory of the uncorruptible God into an image made like to corruptible man, and to birds, and fourfooted beasts, and creeping things. Wherefore God also gave them up to uncleanness through the lusts of their own hearts, to dishonour their own bodies between themselves (Rom. 1:21-24).

Dr. Zaki Y. Saad described some of the gods of ancient Egypt from a cylindrical seal discovered at the Helwan excavations:

> On it is incised the figure of a man whose head resembles that of a bird with a long beak. The three fingers on each hand resemble talons. Beside the man are two giraffes facing one another. . . . In front of the giraffe on the left is the sign of the god Min; above it is the representation of what appears to be a crocodile. Above the giraffe

on the right is the representation of a falcon . . . holding a mace and
a shield. The entire group evidently represents the name of King
Aha, the second king of the First Dynasty.

It is evident that the first people in the land of Egypt changed
the image of God into something resembling four-footed beasts,
birds, and creeping things. And if Enoch was the builder of the
first pyramid, the Great Pyramid, then the spiritual truths embodied within it were corrupted in the lesser pyramids and
tombs. Enoch was translated so that he would not see death,
and the patriarch's escape from death could have prompted others to attempt to duplicate his translation. This may seem at first
a rather unfounded assumption, but there was something mysterious about the embalming process by which the Egyptians
mummified the bodies of their dead.

According to the *Encyclopaedia Britannica*, the process of
mummification of the dead dates to the first dynasty, over 3000
B.C. By the fifth dynasty, the process of preserving the bodies of
the dead had been perfected. All internal organs were removed,
including the brain. The body was then washed and put into a
salt solution for a period of weeks, during which the fatty tis-
sues that were left would be dissolved. Then the body was dried
in the sun, and then returned to a natural appearance by rub-
bing with resin. Resin was probably extracted from pine or ce-
dar trees in Lebanon, and resin was thought to be the blood of
the Egyptian god Osiris. Finally, the body was wrapped and put
into a coffer and/or tomb. Some animals that the Egyptians
thought sacred, or associated with the gods, were also mummified. There is no evidence that bitumen or any other oil sub-
stances were used in the process, and neither Herodotus or
Siculus made any notation that they were used.

Suggestions have been offered that pyramid-shaped structures were used in the mummification procedure, and claims

have been made that animals and birds found in pyramids have been mummified—thus, the connection with pyramid-shaped tombs for the dead. In the 1960s and '70s a pyramid fad surged through several countries, including the United States. Claims were made that pyramid-shaped tents (solid structures, or even cardboard pyramids) had mystical powers. Milk did not sour in such geometric figures, razor blades were resharpened, and the flavors of foods were enhanced. Some even wore pyramid-shaped hats to get rid of headaches. Karl Drabal was granted a patent for a styrofoam model of his pyramid by the Czechoslovakian government under patent number 91304. It was manufactured by a Czech firm, and evidently there was considerable demand for this product. It does seem evident that ancient peoples associated the shape of the pyramid with immortality, because not only did Egyptians bury their kings in pyramidal-shaped buildings, but so did the Chinese, Chaldeans, Mayans of South America and Central America, as well as other cultures.

The main reason Egyptians mummified their dead was they believed that when the spirit returned at the time of the resurrection it would have to recognize the body to which it belonged. And although it did not attain to immortality as believed, it did attain another type of immortality. Scientists and anthropologists delving into the hidden mysteries of the Egyptians who had attained a degree of civilization unparalleled in history, have taken DNA samples from the mummies in the tombs. They have found that members of the royal families married members of other royal families and never married commoners, even if they had to marry cousins or immediate family members. Hatshepsut married her much younger brother, or half-brother, just to assure her claim to be queen. Her brother, in turn, hated her so much that after her death he defaced her figures in her mausoleum, statues in Karnak, and erased every mention of her in the chronicles of Egypt. So mummification has, in the long term, served a valuable historical purpose, even though it made no contribution to eternal life in the resurrection of the dead.

But we read of the translation of Enoch from mortal existence to a state of immortality in Hebrews 11:5-6:

> By faith Enoch was translated that he should not see death; and was not found, because God had translated him: for before his translation he had this testimony, that he pleased God. But without faith it is impossible to please him: for he that cometh to God must believe that he is, and that he is a rewarder of them that diligently seek him.

Man escapes from the penalty of eternal death to eternal life only by faith in God's atonement for sin, and that atonement is in the person of the Lord Jesus Christ, who died in the sinner's place. Cain and Abel both offered a sacrifice for sin. The difference between their sacrifices was that Abel offered up a lamb, a symbol of his faith in the atonement that God would provide for his sins in the person of God's Son. Cain's sacrifice was a symbol of Cain's determination to do something in his own strength. Both believed in the existence of God and both believed they needed redemption from sin. They simply went about it in different ways. Abel who went by the way of faith, was saved, but Cain, who went by the way of his own works, was lost.

Enoch was translated by faith, and this is the spiritual lesson which the Great Pyramid illustrates. However, like the Egyptians, others also went the way of Cain. God has said to sinful man, ". . . dust thou art, and unto dust shalt thou return." The mummification of the dead was man's way of bypassing this Divine edict. No civilization believed in life after death more strongly than the Egyptians, and no other race or nation of people made more preparations for life after death. But the mummies of their dead and the articles they stored in their tombs bear testimony that, like Cain, they believed they could attain immortality by their own knowledge and strength. They believed the Devil's lie: "Ye shall not surely die . . . ye shall be as gods."

Egypt has always been a land of strange contradictions. In spite of all the idolatry and cruelty of the Egyptians, Abraham found refuge in Egypt and was treated kindly by the Pharaoh. Joseph rose to a place of prominence in Egypt, and his father and all his brothers were given food, shelter, and good land when they fled to Egypt to escape from the famine. Although a later Pharaoh enslaved the children of Israel and committed terrible atrocities against them, it was to this same land that Joseph took Jesus, our Lord and Savior, to hide Him from the wrath of Herod. And among the greatest contradictions in the history of Egypt is the Great Pyramid and the lesser pyramids. The Great Pyramid with its empty coffer and missing capstone speaks of a resurrection and immortal life through faith in the capstone of God's spiritual house: the Lord Jesus Christ. The lesser pyramids speak of the futility of man's attempt to attain immortality through his own works.

Chapter Five

The Stone Rejected by the Builders

The Old Testament makes many references to the "cornerstone" of the world. In Job 38:6–7, we read:

> Whereupon are the foundations thereof fastened? or who laid the corner stone thereof; When the morning stars sang together, and all the sons of God shouted for joy?

Likewise in Psalm 118:21–24 it says:

> I will praise thee: for thou hast heard me, and art become my salvation. The stone which the builders refused is become the head stone of the corner. This is the LORD's doing; it is marvellous in our eyes. This is the day which the LORD hath made; we will rejoice and be glad in it.

And in Isaiah 28:16 we read:

> Therefore thus saith the Lord GOD, Behold, I lay in Zion for a foundation a stone, a tried stone, a precious corner stone, a sure foundation: he that believeth shall not make haste.

What did God tell Job when He made reference to the cornerstone of the world? And why did all the sons of God shout for joy when the cornerstone was selected? What did the psalmist mean when he prophesied that the cornerstone would be rejected by the builders? And why did Isaiah make a subsequent prophecy that the cornerstone which the builders of Israel rejected would eventually be laid in Zion?

The New Testament answers these questions for us. In Matthew 21:42 Jesus identified Himself as the cornerstone which the leaders of Israel had rejected. This is also affirmed in 1 Peter 2:4–8:

> To whom coming, as unto a living stone, disallowed indeed of men, but chosen of God, and precious, Ye also, as lively stones, are built up a spiritual house, an holy priesthood, to offer up spiritual sacrifices, acceptable to God by Jesus Christ. Wherefore also it is contained in the scripture, Behold, I lay in Sion a chief corner stone, elect, precious: and he that believeth on him shall not be confounded. Unto you therefore which believe he is precious: but unto them which be disobedient, the stone which the builders disallowed, the same is made the head of the corner, And a stone of stumbling, and a rock of offence, even to them which stumble at the word, being disobedient: whereunto also they were appointed.

Likewise, in Luke 20:17–18:

> And he beheld them, and said, What is this then that is written, The stone which the builders rejected, the same is become the head of the corner? Whosoever shall fall upon that stone shall be broken; but on whomsoever it shall fall, it will grind him to powder.

Each stone that was used in the construction of the Great Pyramid had to be precisely fitted into place. If a stone was brought up and would not fit, or if it was of inferior quality, the builders would reject it, push it over the side to go plummeting down to the baseline. Whosoever got in the way of one of these huge stones would be smashed to bits. If any merely slipped and fell on the stones, they might receive only broken bones, but if any of the stones fell upon the workmen, they would be ground to powder.

There is only one type of building in all the world that requires a head cornerstone: a pyramid. But there is no head cornerstone on the top of the Great Pyramid. It would be utterly inconceivable for Cheops, or some other great king or religious leader to spend many years and vast sums of money to construct such an edifice, and then leave it uncapped. It would appear that a headstone in which all the corners would merge was prepared, but was rejected by the builders. And thus no other building in all the world, except the Great Pyramid, fits the symbolism of the unfinished building described in the Old Testament and completed in the New.

We read of the Kingdom of God which the redeemed will inherit in Hebrews 4:3: ". . . the works were finished from the foundation of the world." Jesus said in Matthew 25:34:

> Then shall the King say unto them on his right hand, Come, ye blessed of my Father, inherit the kingdom prepared for you from the foundation of the world.

This Kingdom is compared to a house or a building of stones like the Great Pyramid. When it is completed, it will be the head cornerstone, Jesus Christ, who will do it. The capstone of this building of God was chosen from before the foundation of the world (1 Pet. 1:20; Rev. 13:8).

This is why we read in Job 38:6–7: ". . . Or who laid the cornerstone thereof; When the morning stars sang together, and all the sons of God shouted for joy?" When God revealed to the angels His plan of creating mankind a holy habitation to be crowned with the precious cornerstone of His only begotten Son, there was ecstasy in Heaven. The morning stars sang together, and the angels shouted for joy, and we read in Luke 15:7,10, that there is still joy in Heaven over one sinner who repents, because the sooner the building is completed, the sooner the cornerstone will be fitted to the building and Christ will be all in all.

This heavenly blueprint is beautifully illustrated in the design of the Great Pyramid, and many outstanding Bible scholars like Clarence Larkin and Dr. J. A. Seiss have described it as a Bible in stone. Quoting Larkin:

> The Great Pyramid is the only form of building that conforms to the symbolic description of the **spiritual building** spoken of in Scripture, of which Christ is said to be the **chief cornerstone**. Eph. 2:20–22, "And are built upon the foundation of the apostles and prophets, Jesus Christ himself being the chief corner stone; In whom all the building fitly framed together groweth unto an holy temple in the Lord: In whom ye also are builded together for an habitation of God through the Spirit." There is no **chief cornerstone** in architectural construction, but in a building of pyramidal form, and in shape it is exactly like the building it tops out. To its angles **all the buildings fitly framed together.** Being five-sided, there is no place for it in the building until the finishing touch is given, and therefore the builders rejected it until needed. So we read of Christ—"The stone which the builders disallowed . . . the same is made the head of the corner. And a stone of stumbling, and a rock of offence"! The capstone of a pyramid until needed would be in the way, and a "stone of stumbling" and "a rock of offence" to the workmen. So with Christ. Paul says—"We preach Christ crucified, unto the Jews a stumbling-block, and unto the Greeks foolishness," or, "rock of offence" (1 Cor. 1:23). The capstone of a pyramid is five sided and five pointed, with sharp points always sticking up. Anyone falling on it would be "broken" or injured, and when on its way to its lofty position, were

it to fall on anyone, it would "grind him to powder." From what has been said we see that the Great Pyramid is symbolic of the Spiritual Building of which Christ is the "Chief Capstone."

It would also be well for us to consider the opinion of Dr. J. A. Seiss, the dean of modern pre-millennial scholars, concerning the Great Pyramid:

> Egypt was a hotbed of idolatry from the beginning. Its people began by the worship of heroes and heavenly bodies, and ended in the worship of bulls, cats, crocodiles, hawks, and beetles. Their false religion was in full sway when Cheops was born. Lepsius tells us that the whole land was full of temples, filled with statues of kings and gods, their walls within and without covered with colored reliefs and hieroglyphics in celebration of the virtues of their hero gods and their divine and ever-faultless children. Nothing, even down to the palette of a painter, the style with which a lady tinted her eyelashes, or a walking stick, was deemed too insignificant to be inscribed with the name of the owner, and a votive dedication of the object to some patron divinity. And yet, here is the Great Pyramid, the largest, finest, and most wonderful edifice in all Egypt, situated in the midst of an endless round of tombs, temples, and monuments, all uniformly loaded down with these idolatrous emblems and inscriptions, and in all its long avenues, Grand Gallery and exquisite chambers, in any department or place whatever, there has never been found one ancient inscription or slightest sign of Egypt's idolatry! In the center of the intensest impurity, the Great Pyramid stands without spot, blemish, or remotest taint of the surrounding flood of abominations, like the incarnate Son of God, sinless in a world of sinners.

A subterranean chamber is sunk deep in the rock below the base of the pyramid and is representative of Hell, the bottomless pit

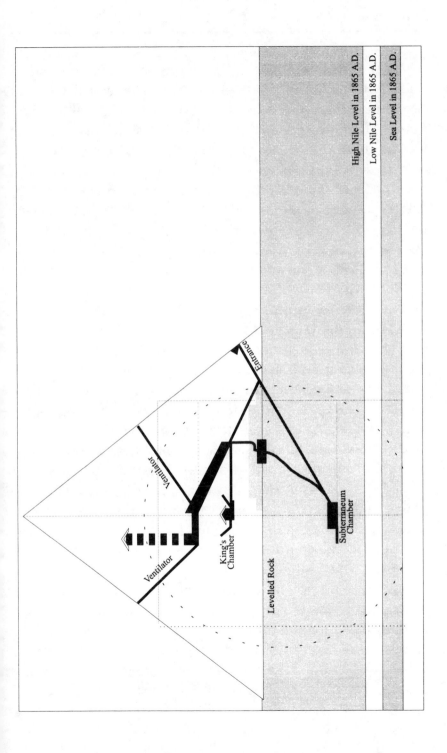

Ventilator

Ventilator

King's Chamber

Entrance

Subterraneum Chamber

Levelled Rock

High Nile Level in 1865 A.D.

Low Nile Level in 1865 A.D.

Sea Level in 1865 A.D.

where the Devil will be chained during our Lord's millennial reign. But after the one thousand-year reign has ended, Hell will be removed from its position and cast into the lake of fire (Rev. 20:14). There would appear to be no possible reason for the builders of the Great Pyramid to have carved out a pit unless it were to depict the reality of Hell.

All religions propose their own concepts of Heaven and Hell. Adherents work to get to Heaven or stay out of Hell. Christians neither work to go to Heaven nor to escape Hell. Salvation is by faith in Jesus Christ, not of works (Eph. 2:8-9). Christianity is not a religion; it is a relationship with God as His family, His children, whereby we become heirs with Jesus Christ.

On a mission trip to China in 1987, as we usually do, we sailed down the Yangtze River. One of our stops was Fengdu. A river ship stopping at that town was a tremendous event, and there were thousands at the dock. Being in the backwoods, and out of reach of government agents, we felt at liberty to distribute Bibles and tracts. Within minutes all was gone as thousands of hands reached out for whatever we had to offer.

This town was located at the base of a high, cone-shaped, mountain. On top of the mountain was a Buddhist shrine named, "999 Steps to Hell." It was about a three-mile climb to the top, and along the way there were nine hundred and ninety-nine steps. At the top, in a large pit, was the Buddhist conception of Hell. Mannequins appearing as demons with horns and pitchforks were beating, torturing, and casting the damned into fires of eternal torment. In the pit also were thousands upon thousands of Chinese currency bills. The poor Chinese Buddhists were casting money into the pit to lessen their judgment in Hell. This monetary sacrifice was even more impressive considering the wage of a commune worker is only $15.00 a month. This sad example, however, should make the salvation for the Christian made possible by Jesus' sacrifice on the cross even more wonderful and precious: "Forasmuch as ye know that ye were not redeemed with corruptible things, as silver and gold . . . But with the precious blood of Christ, as of a lamb without blemish and without spot" (1 Pet. 1:18–19).

At the north face of the Great Pyramid, fifteen levels above the base, is the only entrance. Huge plates of granite stone, weighing at least ten tons each, form the symmetrical doorway. The architecture resembles that of the queen's tomb at Ur that is reckoned to be of pre-flood vintage. The entrance was actually constructed inside the pyramid, leaving no outward sign of a door. For centuries treasure seekers and robbers searched for the entrance. One Al Mamoun did start at the fifth level in about the year A.D. 825. Mamoun was a Moslem caliph from Arabia. For days and weeks his men chiseled through solid stone. After advancing painstakingly in the desert heat through forty feet of almost solid stone, they were about to give up when they heard a stone fall. This encouraged the would-be robbers, and with dreams of gold, silver, and precious stones in their heads, they redoubled their efforts and finally entered an open space where the ascending and descending passages intersected. With their torches they rushed up the ascending passage, bending at the knees because it is only approximately four feet high, and finally entered the Grand Gallery. On they went through the King's Antechamber and entered the Throne Room, which is about the size of a dining room or small bedroom. It was a beautiful room of polished red granite with a burial coffer, also of red granite, but nothing else, not even hieroglyphics on the walls. I have made the journey up through the ascending passageway, through the Grand Gallery, and into the Throne Room many times. The beautiful red coffer, placed in the middle of the Throne Room, is still there. And I can imagine at first the unbelief, then frustration, and then the anger that the workers must have experienced. There is a large piece of the coffer missing from one corner, and it could be that in their frustration, Al Mamoun's men attacked it and broke off this one segment; or perhaps Napoleon, or some other pyramid visitor, took home this piece of the Great Pyramid as a souvenir.

As we look at the overall design of the Great Pyramid, we must wonder why the builder, or builders, would have constructed a descending passage of 370 feet, 275 feet through a solid rock base, to create a subterranean chamber. If Josephus, and others whom we have noted, agree that the Great Pyramid is a Bible in stone, the subterranean chamber must represent Hades, or to the Egyptians, the underworld. Immediately upon entering at the door the visitor goes down the descending passage on the way to the subterranean chamber. This could speak to us of the truth that all men are born in sin on the way to Hell. However, after descending approximately eighty-five feet, which correspondingly would be the age of accountability of twelve years, the visitor reaches an intersection with an ascending passageway. Now, he must choose which way to go—down or up. The ascending passageway is small, but Jesus said, "I am the way, the truth, and the life, no man cometh unto the Father but by me," but that way is very narrow—only "by me." Now after the visitor chooses to go up the ascending passages, he comes to the Grand Gallery. No longer does he have to stoop, crawl, or grovel—it is long, high, and ascending. At the entrance to the Grand Gallery is a descending passage into the pit, with another intersecting passage leading to the Queen's Room. The Queen is, of course, the bride of the King. So now the visitor passes the last trip leading to the pit, where he is a member of the Queen's company, which represents the Church, and he can now rush past the Antechamber into the presence of the King Himself.

We understand that some will conclude that we are reaching for straws in attempting to read something into the Great Pyramid that is not there. However, Isaiah certainly indicated that the Great Pyramid was a pillar, or altar, to the Lord. An altar is where men and women offer a sacrifice, whether it is themselves or a substitute animal, in order to meet God. Of course, we know that Jesus Christ was our sacrifice, once and for all. Nevertheless, if the Word of God signifies the Great Pyramid as an altar, then our humble comparisons should have some merit and acknowledge a measure of credibility.

The stone which the builders, meaning Israel, rejected, has become the cornerstone of our salvation, and according to Daniel 2:44–45, will stand forever and fill the whole Earth.

Chapter Six

The Empty Coffer

At the end of the Grand Gallery where it terminates at the fiftieth level of masonry, there is a low level entrance into a room identified as the King's Antechamber. The antechamber is where those wishing an audience with the king wait to be summoned. From the antechamber there is another entrance leading to a larger room, the King's Chamber. The entrance leading from the antechamber to the King's Chamber is three and one-half feet high, three and one-half feet wide, and approximately eight and one-half feet long. A visitor being granted an audience with the king would enter, whether willing or not, either in a crawling or bowing position.

After passing through the entrance, the visitor enters into a large room thirty-four feet long, seventeen feet wide, and nineteen feet high. The combined dimensions are seventy feet which corresponds to man's expected life-span (Ps. 90:10). The room is finished in beautiful polished pink granite. To protect the room from being imploded by the tremendous weight above, the builders used massive granite beams, weighing fifty to seventy tons each, at spaced intervals, totaling a distance of approximately forty feet above. Above the five beams, the architect built into the construction two massive polished beams to meet at forty-five degree angles. Much knowledge of stone construction was required to determine just how to protect the King's Chamber. And though through approximately fifty centuries of holding up millions of tons of weight, and withstanding at least one earthquake a century, and even though the protecting massive beams may have cracked, the King's Chamber remains in perfect condition. There is not a single crack in the walls, floor, or ceiling. What architect today would dare propose a blueprint for a building that would endure five thousand years under such weight?

Within the King's Chamber there is only one item of furnishing—a coffer or sarcophagus. In the pharaohs' tombs at the Valley of the Kings, the mummy was usually enclosed in several coffers. The coffers that held the mummy Tutankhamen are on display at the Cairo Museum. However, in the King's Chamber of the Great Pyramid, there is only one coffer. This coffer was fashioned from a large block of red granite. The dimensions are as follows:

	Length	Breadth	Height	Volume
Interior	77.85	26.70	34.31	71,317
Exterior	89.62	38.61	41.13	142,316

It is evident that the coffer would have accommodated the body of a man six feet tall, even with the wrapping and mask that were placed on the body after mummification. According to George Riffert in his book, Great Pyramid of God (p. 33), in pyramid inches the volume would be 71,250 square inches. The common concept that most Christians have of the Ark of the Covenant is that it was a modest chest, perhaps the size of a foot locker, that was highly polished and overlaid with gold. However, this is not what the Scriptures indicate. We read in Exodus 25:10: "And they shall make an ark of shittim wood: two cubits and a half shall be the length thereof, and a cubit and a half the breadth thereof, and a cubit and a half the height thereof."

The Ark of the Covenant was the size of an average coffin, and we believe this is what it was to represent. Inside the Ark were the tablets of the law. The law condemned, it did not save. The law revealed the exceeding sinfulness of sin. By the law was no flesh saved from death. The soul that sinneth, it shall die, was the message of the Ark. Redemption from this penalty was only through the blood, and the sprinkling of the blood upon the Mercy Seat, or the lid of the Ark, acknowledged faith in the Redeemer who would come and shed His blood and overcome death and Hell. The Ark of the Covenant pointed Israel to Romans 11:27: "For this is my covenant unto them, when I shall take away their sins." The Ark of the Covenant pointed forward to the Messiah who would take the curse of the law upon Himself, and remove the sting of the law, as we read in 1 Corinthians 15:24–26; 55–57,

> Then cometh the end, when he shall have delivered up the kingdom to God, even the Father; when he shall have put down all rule and all authority and power. For he must reign, till he hath put all enemies under his feet. The last enemy that shall be destroyed is death. . . . O death, where is thy sting? O grave, where is thy victory? The sting of death is sin; and the strength of sin is the law. But thanks be to God, which giveth us the victory through our Lord Jesus Christ.

There is much conjecture as to what happened to the Ark of the Covenant. In the Apocrypha it is indicated that Jeremiah hid the Ark on Mt. Nebo; others believe it was taken to Ethiopia, and still others believe it is hidden under the Temple site on Mt. Moriah. I personally do not believe the Ark will be found until after the Church is raptured, because today we are under grace and not law.

The Temple was a picture, or type, of the spiritual Temple of

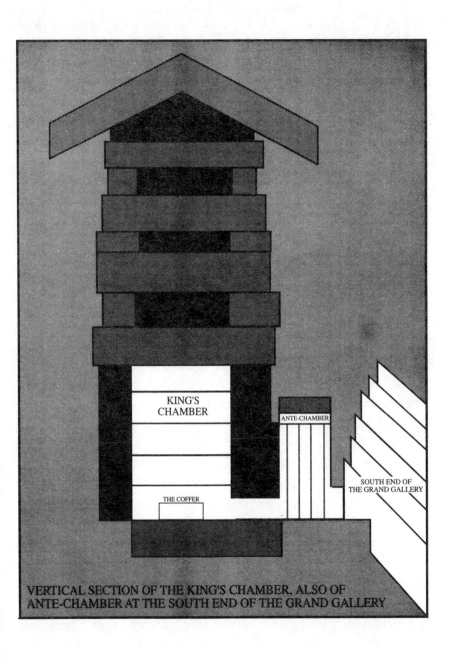

KING'S
CHAMBER

ANTE-CHAMBER

SOUTH END OF
THE GRAND GALLERY

THE COFFER

VERTICAL SECTION OF THE KING'S CHAMBER, ALSO OF
ANTE-CHAMBER AT THE SOUTH END OF THE GRAND GALLERY

God in Heaven, just as the Ark was also a type of the true Ark of God in Heaven. Only the high priest saw the Ark, and he lived only by the shed blood of an animal, a type of the blood that Jesus Christ was to shed to satisfy the justice demanded by the law. The Ark of God, in Heaven, likewise is a symbol of God's judgment against sin, as demanded by the law of God. We read in Revelation 11:18–19:

> And the nations were angry, and thy wrath is come, and the time of the dead, that they should be judged, and that thou shouldest give reward unto thy servants the prophets, and to the saints, and them that fear thy name, small and great; and shouldest destroy them which destroy the earth. And the temple of God was opened in heaven, and there was seen in his temple the ark of his testament: and there were lightnings, and voices, and thunderings, and an earthquake, and great hail.

Again we see the Ark as a symbol of judgment for sin, a symbol of death, a coffin for all who die in their sins without redemption. Perhaps it is no coincidence that the coffer in the Great Pyramid is the same size as the Ark of the Covenant.

The tomb holding the body of the Lord Jesus Christ was sealed, just as the tomb in the Great Pyramid was sealed. It required weeks of drilling through stone before Al Mamoun and his men broke into an open passageway. When they finally broke into the King's Chamber, they found the coffer empty and not even one piece of gold or a single precious stone.

Likewise, when Jesus returned to Heaven he left no earthly possessions. He said that He didn't even have a place to lay His head. And why did the builders of the Great Pyramid select granite with a red color rather than yellow, gray, or black? Again we marvel at the typology and try to understand the complete meaning of Jeremiah's and Isaiah's pronouncements that God had established wonders in Egypt and His pillar in the midst of that land.

Chapter Seven

The 144,000 Casing Blocks

The outward appearance of the Great Pyramid today is rather rough and unsightly, but this was not always the case. Before 1517 the Great Pyramid was covered with polished, white limestone casing blocks. It was in that year that the Turks expanded their empire over Egypt. The beautiful casing blocks were removed for building purposes. The most common estimate of the number of casing blocks it required to cover the twenty square acres of the pyramid's four faces is 144,000.

Herodotus wrote that visitors, when approaching from the west, or the east, over the desert, could see the Great Pyramid for miles before arriving at Cairo. The historian noted that the Great Pyramid appeared as a building let down from Heaven. Each limestone casing block was cut to an exact standard, so it is relatively easy to calculate how many blocks it would require to cover twenty acres—144,000. Sir Flanders Petrie, British archaeologist, stated of the casing stones:

> These joints, with an area of some 35 square feet each, were not only worked as finely as this, but were cemented throughout. Though the stones were brought as close as 1/500th part of an inch, or in fact, into contact and the mean opening of the joint was but 1/50th part of an inch, yet the builders managed to fill the joint with cement. . . . Merely to place such stones in each contact would be careful work, but to do so with cement in the joints seems to us

almost impossible. Their almost superhuman skill in fixing in position and cementing the joints of such immense stones is indeed difficult to understand. How, in the casing of the Great Pyramid they could fill with cement a vertical joint almost five feet by seven feet in area, with surfaces practically in contact is a mystery. . . . Yet this was the usual work over twenty acres of surface, with tens of thousands of casing stones.

Sir Petrie added his own opinion to that of others that the Great Pyramid was created by abilities beyond human means. But why the 144,000 white limestone casing blocks? We are told in Revelation 7 that before any judgments of the Great Tribulation are to begin, twelve thousand out of each of the twelve tribes of Israel will be sealed. Each tribe is named, and the roster includes Joseph. The tribes of Ephraim and Dan are omitted. Ephraim mixed with other people and Dan lacked the faith to claim the portion of land God gave him.

The 144,000 sealed Israelites are to be witnesses for God during the Great Tribulation. If the Church was still in the world, then God would not have to call and seal 144,000 Israelites. We believe the Church will be raptured, or translated to Heaven, before the Tribulation begins. We realize that there is a considerable variance of opinions on this point of eschatology.

Herodotus indicated the Great Pyramid (before the white limestone covering blocks were removed) looked like a building let down from Heaven. We are told that Abraham looked for a city whose builder and maker was God, the New Jerusalem. We know that Abraham went to Egypt, and we might wonder if he had not heard of the Great Pyramid and had gone to see if this was the city the Lord promised. Some Bible scholars believe that the New Jerusalem will be in the form of a pyramid. As we consider the Great Pyramid, we see the King's Chamber, the Queen's Chamber, Israel as the lively stones in 1 Peter 2:5, and the 144,000 saved Israelites of the Tribulation. The only thing that is missing is the capstone, or Jesus Christ, as we read in 1 Peter 2:6–8, but we know the capstone will be in place when the Lord returns.

Some attempt to explain away or spiritualize the prophecy of the 144,000 sealed Israelites by pointing out that Israeli genealogical records have been lost, and the only identifiable Israelis today by tribe are the priests (Cohens) and the Levites (those who have Levi in their family name). We have already referred to the identity of the royal families of Egypt through DNA testing, even those who have been dead for five thousand years. In 1917 the family of Czar Nicholas of Russia was massacred. The communist assassins at first buried the bodies. Later the Romanoffs were dug up, their bodies burned into ash, and then their bones were thrown into a swamp. After more than seventy-five years the remains of the bones were located. DNA testing on the bones proved the identity of each member, with the exception of one female child, Anastasia. Her bones were missing, but it had been rumored for years that Anastasia escaped and lived in New York City under an assumed name. So DNA identification testing is accepted by the scientific world as absolute proof—the only exception being the O. J. Simpson jury.

In 1976 Professor Arthur Koestler published a 240-page book through Random House of New York titled, *The Thirteenth Tribe*. Koestler contends that the Ashkenazi Jews of Israel, as well as the rest of the world, are the descendants of the Kazar people who lived between the Black Sea and the Caspian Sea in southern Russia. In about A.D. 750 the Judaic religion did make deep inroads into the Kazar population. In subsequent wars between the Moslem and Christian worlds, as well as the Mongol invasion, Koestler claims that the Kazars left their homeland and settled in Poland, and the Ashkenazi Jews are not really Jews. In conclusion, Koestler contended in his book that the myth of the

Jews as a chosen race of people by God was proven false. Many have used this book with its conclusions to promote anti-Semitism and reject Israel's right to exist as a nation.

When I studied the history of both the Kazars and the Ashkenazi Jews, as well as the Sephardic Jews, I totally rejected Koestler's theory as false scholarship. Now it seems that microbiology has proven Koestler to be in error. We quote from a UPI science report dated January 30, 1995:

> An examination of the gene that causes a movement disorder indicates that the world's 12 million Ashkenazi Jews originated from a few thousand centered in Russia and Poland 500 to 600 years ago, researchers said Monday. The Yale University researchers analyzed a specific genetic mutation that is common among Ashkenazi Jews and concluded that the population had expanded from 3,000 in the 16th century to over 5 million in 1990. . . . Of the 14 million Jews in the world today, nearly 80 percent are Ashkenazim—a Hebrew word meaning German. The Ashkenazi originated in Israel, migrated to the Rhineland in the 9th century, and starting in the 14th century settled in present-day Poland, Lithuania, the Ukraine, and Russia.

The genetic trait of the Ashkenazi Jews reveals they came out of Israel at the beginning of the Diaspora, settled in Germany, then migrated to Poland and Russia, and not in the reverse as Koestler claims. They are indeed Jews according to genealogies, scientifically proven. Previously, the only way it could be proven as to which tribe Jews belonged was by fragmented migration records and by family name, like Cohen or Levi. We read in Revelation 7 that during the Tribulation period God will seal twelve thousand out of each of the twelve tribes of Israel. In Ezekiel 48 the inheritance of the twelve tribes of Israel in the Millennium is given. The puzzle has been, which Jews belong to which tribe? We suggest it might even be possible to solve this riddle through the developing science of genetic DNA microbiology.

Joseph gave instructions to bury his bones in Israel when his people returned to the Promised Land. The bones of the prophets are buried in tombs, and in ossuary boxes on the western side of the Mt. of Olives. The ossuary box containing the bones of the high priest Caiaphas was discovered in 1994. Without doubt, the bones of a representative from each of the tribes of Israel could be located.

We do not say without qualification that this is the way the 144,000 sealed Israelites will be identified according to tribe, but it is worth considering. Nevertheless, it is God who will do the sealing. God has foretold that at the end of the Tribulation He will bring every Jew in the world back into the land of Israel. Even if any Jews are in a space vehicle in outer space, God will bring them back (Neh. 1:9). If God knows the racial identity of every Israelite, He can know their tribal indentification also.

As we look to Israel today and see yeshivas near the Western Wall weaving priest's clothing out of pure linen according to biblical specifications, Cohens being trained to administer services in the Temple, articles of furnishings and vessels for Temple worship services being made ready, we know that the time for the sealing of the 144,000 must be at hand. Therefore, we see the blueprint for God's eternal New Jerusalem, as revealed in His Word, and in type in the Great Pyramid, beginning to take shape.

> Now therefore ye are no more strangers and foreigners, but fellow-citizens with the saints, and of the household of God; And are built upon the foundation of the apostles and prophets, Jesus Christ himself being the chief corner stone; In whom all the building fitly framed together groweth unto an holy temple in the Lord: In whom ye also are builded together for an habitation of God through the Spirit (Eph. 2:19–22).

Chapter Eight

Countdown 2000

For I testify unto every man that heareth the words of the prophecy of this book, If any man shall add unto these things, God shall add unto him the plagues that are written in this book: And if any man shall take away from the words of the book of this prophecy, God shall take away his part out of the book of life, and out of the holy city, and from the things which are written in this book (Rev. 22:18–19).

In eschatology we cannot add anything to that which God has prophesied in the Scriptures. Everything we need to know about the future is in the Bible. Our responsibility is to compare world events on the national, international, economic, political, environmental, and ecclesiastical planes with the Word of prophecy to determine where we are on God's prophetic clock. The Great Pyramid cannot add anything to the written Word; it can only verify in type that which God has purposed for the ages to come.

Before we get into a study of prophecy in stone, we need to be brought forward along the prophetic scale to the present in order to determine if the prophetic projections that some see in the Great Pyramid are valid, or even credible.

But when the fulness of the time was come, God sent forth his Son, made of a woman, made under the law (Gal. 4:4).

A noted scholar of the Greek language, Dr. Kenneth Wuest, commented on this verse:

> The meaning is that when that moment came which completed the period of time designated by God that should elapse before the coming of the Son of God in incarnation, then He would send forth His Son. . . . It was the moment which God had ordained for Messiah's coming. To Daniel was given the date of His coming, 483 years after the edict of the Medo-Persian government to rebuild Jerusalem (Dan. 9:25–27).

God preordained the moment that Jesus Christ was to be born. According to *Ussher's Chronology*, it was four thousand years (and we believe to the very second) after life was given to the first man, Adam. Four is the number of the world, and Jesus Christ came to save the world (John 3:17).

God the Father also has a preordained time for the Second Coming of Jesus Christ: "But of that day and hour knoweth no man, no, not the angels of heaven, but my Father only" (Matt. 24:36). No man or no angel can know the exact day, or time of day, Jesus will come back. All attempts by so-called prophetic scholars to date the exact time that Jesus will leave the throne of God to return to planet Earth are in vain. To conclude otherwise would make Jesus Christ a false prophet.

The knowledge of the time of Christ's return is further qualified in Mark 13:32: "But of that day and that hour knoweth no man, no, not the angels which are in heaven, neither the Son, but the Father." So even Jesus does not know the day or the hour that He will come back.

The prophetic Word would have made things much simpler if the Scriptures had stated that no man, no angel, or even the Son, can know the hour, the day, the month, the year, or the century that Jesus will return, but the Scriptures do not say this.

They only limit our foreknowledge by speaking of the day and the hour, even though some may contend that a much longer period of time is implied. However, the error in our calendar, from one to four years, probably takes care of the annual qualification, at least up to four years.

The evident reason that Jesus did not go beyond limiting knowledge of His return to longer than one day is that not only can Christians know when His return would be near, it would be their responsibility to know. We do not wish to even imply that knowledge of Christ's return can be pinpointed to within one day, but it is possible to determine by the signs of the times when His coming is near: "So likewise ye, when ye shall see all these things, know that it is near, even at the doors" (Matt. 24:33).

> And when these things begin to come to pass, then look up, and lift up your heads; for your redemption draweth nigh. . . . So likewise ye, when ye see these things come to pass, know ye that the kingdom of God is nigh at hand (Luke 21:28,31).

> Knowing this first, that there shall come in the last days scoffers, walking after their own lusts, And saying, Where is the promise of his coming? . . . (2 Pet. 3:3–4).

> But ye, brethren, are not in darkness, that that day should overtake you as a thief (1 Thess. 5:4).

Matthew, from the Jewish position that would exist in the Great Tribulation, indicated that the Jews could know that the coming of Messiah, Jesus Christ, was *even at the doors.* Luke, from a comprehensive standpoint, indicated that anyone, Jew or Gentile, could know from the signs of the times that the Lord's coming was *near.*

Peter and Paul encourage evangelism as the Day of the Lord

becomes evident from the fulfilling of prophetic signs. The redemption or translation of the Church (Rapture) occurs before the Tribulation. Therefore, *Christians are encouraged to look for signs of the coming Antichrist and the Tribulation period.*

Why 2000?

For reasons why the year A.D. 2000 is creating messianic expectations, let us consider the internal evidence of Scripture. The number one sign of the appearance of the Kingdom Age, the coming of Messiah to bring down the Kingdom of Heaven on Earth, would be the return of the Jews (Israelites) from all nations. This sign was foretold by the prophets from Moses to Jesus Christ. While Daniel's seventy prophetic weeks tell us in the first sixty-nine weeks (interpreted to be four hundred and eighty-three years) how long it would be before the Messiah would come and then be cut off (crucified), the prophet was not told how long the breach between the sixty-ninth and seventieth weeks would be. It would be at the end of the seventieth week (the last seven years of the four hundred and ninety-year prophetic period) that all the promises of God to Israel would be realized and fulfilled. That Israel would be dispersed into all nations is clearly prophesied (Deut. 28:25). That the breach between God and Israel would cease at the end of the seventieth week of Daniel (the Tribulation period) is also clearly foretold in Deuteronomy 30:3, Isaiah 30:19, and many other Scriptures. However, only Hosea provided information concerning the length of the breach, or the Diaspora:

> For the children of Israel shall abide many days without a king, and without a prince, and without a sacrifice, and without an image, and without an ephod, and without teraphim: Afterward shall the children of Israel return, and seek the LORD their God, and David their

king; and shall fear the Lᴏʀᴅ and his goodness *in the latter days*. . . . I will go and return to my place, till they acknowledge their offence, and seek my face: in their affliction they will seek me early. Come, and let us return unto the Lᴏʀᴅ: for he hath torn, and he will heal us; he hath smitten, and he will bind us up. *After two days will he revive us:* in the third day he will raise us up, and we shall live in his sight. Then shall we know, if we follow on to know the Lᴏʀᴅ: his going forth is prepared as the morning; *and he shall come unto us as the rain,* as the latter and former rain unto the earth (Hos. 3:4–5; 5:15; 6:1–3).

It appears rather obvious in cross referencing Psalm 90:4 and 2 Peter 3:8 that the two days in which Israel would be scattered is two thousand years, which is further evidenced by the fact that the Diaspora lasted for two thousand years. Hosea continued to explain that at the end of two days the Lord would come and revive Israel. The prophet also included another clue as to when the Lord would come: He would come as the latter and former rain. The prophet Joel also foretold that when the Lord regathered Israel that He would restore unto the land both the former and the latter rain. In my *Pilgrim Study Bible*, Joel 2:23 carries the following footnote:

> There always used to be two rainy seasons in Palestine, one in the spring, the other in the fall. The second rain God withheld while Israel was scattered, but He promised to send it again about the time when Israel was going to return. It is interesting to note that it began again, lightly, about the beginning of the twentieth century, and has been increasing ever since.

The *Pilgrim Study Bible* was published in 1948. Since 1948 the rainfall in Israel has continued to increase, currently almost doubling the amount since the Jews began returning. When Israel is absent from the land it becomes barren and desolate. Because of the latter rain being restored, the land has once more blossomed as a rose (Isa. 35:1). Also stated explicitly by Hosea and Joel, and implied by Isaiah, Amos, and other prophets, is the promise that when the Jews began to return, *along with the return of the latter rain*, the Messiah would come and fulfill God's covenant with Israel.

An interpretive position relating to the return of Jesus Christ is based on the Genesis' six days of creation. Profound and exhaustive studies involving mathematical designs in the Scriptures show that God, the Master Mathematician, has assigned definitive basic properties to certain numbers, i.e.: two, the number of witnesses; four, the number of the world; six, the number of man (Rev. 13:18); seven, the number of perfection (as on the seventh day when God saw what He had created, and said that "it was very good," meaning "perfect").

God has given man six days, interpreted to mean six millennium, to prove Satan's lie that man can become his own god. The sixth millennium will end in just four years, according to our present calendar, or in 1996 if we consider the calendar error to be four years.

> Wherefore the children of Israel shall keep the sabbath, to observe the sabbath throughout their generations, for a perpetual covenant. It is a sign between me and the children of Israel for ever: for in six days the LORD made heaven and earth, and on the seventh day he rested, and was refreshed (Exod. 31:16–17).

Gentiles were never commanded to keep the Sabbath, because Gentiles apart from God could not keep the Sabbath holy. Unclean Gentiles had no Sabbath, no holy days, no feast days, no Temple, no law, etc. (Eph. 2:11–12). It can be concluded, with some biblical reasoning, that the Sabbath, as kept by Israel, signified that the Kingdom Age, the seventh millennium, would be the Lord's Day that will arrive in just four years according to our calendar. In reference to the seventh day of rest, we read in Hebrews 4:9: "There remaineth therefore a rest to the people of God." The people referred to in Hebrews 4 is Israel, not the Church.

Edward Gibbon finished his monumental historical work, *The Decline and Fall of the Roman Empire*, in 1772. Gibbon was anti-Christian, a friend of Voltaire, yet he presented clearly the pre-millennial doctrine of the early Church that was preached for almost three hundred years after the dispersion of Israel in A.D. 70. We reference the preceding from pages 187–88 of the fifteenth chapter of *The Decline and Fall of the Roman Empire:*

> The revolution of seventeen centuries has instructed us not to press too closely the mysterious language of prophecy and revelation; but as long as, for wise purposes, this error was permitted to subsist in the church, it was produced of the most salutary effects on the faith and practice of Christians, who lived in the awful expectation of that moment when the globe itself, and all the various races of mankind, should tremble at the appearance of their divine Judge. The ancient and popular doctrine of the Millennium was intimately connected with the second coming of Christ. As the works of creation had been finished in six days, their duration in their present state, according to a tradition which was attributed to the prophet Elijah, was fixed to six thousand years. By the same analogy it was inferred that this long period of labour and contention, which was now almost elapsed, would be succeeded by a joyful Sabbath of a thousand years, and that Christ, with the triumphant band of the saints and the elect who had escaped death, or who had been miraculously revived, would reign upon Earth till the time appointed for the last and general resurrection. . . . The assurance of such a Millennium was carefully inculcated by a succession of fathers from Justin Mar-

tyr and Irenaeus, who conversed with the immediate disciples of the apostles, down to Lactanius, who was preceptor to the son of Constantine. Though it might not be universally received, it appears to have been the reigning sentiment of the orthodox believers; and it seems so well adapted to the desires and apprehensions of mankind, that it must have contributed in a very considerable degree to the progress of the Christian faith.

While Edward Gibbon was a critic of the Bible and the Church, he was a good historian, and we are indebted to him for bringing out quite clearly that the early Church fathers taught the pre-millennial return of Jesus Christ with judgment upon the nations to establish His Kingdom upon Earth. Gibbon also indicated that the early Church taught a pre-Tribulation Rapture, as Christ would reign with those believers who "escaped" the Tribulation. Paul in 1 Thessalonians 5 wrote that the "unsaved" would not escape, which means that the saved will escape as presented in 1 Thessalonians 4:13–18.

Gibbon also credits the teaching of the pre-millennial return of Jesus Christ to have contributed to the dissemination of the Gospel and the growth of the Christian faith. After Constantine, the Roman Catholic Church perverted the biblical teachings on the pre-millennial return of Jesus Christ to post-millennial eschatology, meaning that the pope would bring in the Kingdom through the efforts of the Catholic Church.

The World Looks to 2000

While the early Church fathers taught that Jesus Christ would return in the year A.D. 2000 to bring a dramatic dispensational change, many prominent personalities and organizations today expect great dispensational changes in just four years, though not necessarily associated with Christ's return.

The New Age religion teaches that with the dawning of the Age of Aquarius, New Agers will become gods. During the Church Age our sun has been passing through the constellation of Pisces (the Fish). An emblem associated with Christians has been the sign of the fish. With the arrival of the calendar year 2000, the sun will be passing through the constellation of Aquarius, and the New Agers sing, "This is the dawning of the Age of Aquarius," when peace through their own comprehensive false christ will come, and they will rule the planets.

We consider Dr. Malachi Martin to be one of the most intelligent and informed men of this world. He has served in the Vatican and remains a loyal subject of the pope. In his latest book, *The Keys of This Blood*, Dr. Martin indicates that Pope John Paul II believes that by the year 2000 there will be a second Fatima, the Illumination, and all religions will accept him as God's vicar on Earth. In the Sunday, April 3, 1994, edition of *Parade* magazine, Pope John Paul II is quoted as saying:

> We trust that with the approach of the year 2000, Jerusalem will become the city of peace for the entire world and all the people will be able to meet there, in particular the believers in the religions that find their birthright in the faith of Abraham.

The pope hopes that all people will come together in worship in Jerusalem by A.D. 2000, and in particular, adherents to Judaism, Islam, and Christianity (Catholicism and Protestantism). The pope has recently been quoted in the news media as remaining firm in his position that he alone must be the head of any ecumenical religious structure and retain his authority which entails infallibility. Therefore, it seems obvious that the pope expects the great illumination to come in, or before, A.D. 2000 when he will become the head of an international religious entity.

Yasser Arafat, the man who until recently was labeled as one of the most vicious terrorists and murderers of innocent men, women, and children who ever lived, is now himself pointing to the year 2000 as heralding a new era of peace in the world. On November 27, 1995, representatives of twenty-seven nations—nations that were included in the old Roman Empire—met in Barcelona, Spain. The target of the conference was, in Barak of Spain's words, just four years hence:

> Let us not only beat our swords into ploughshares, let us together make swords a tool of the past, make war almost impossible. . . . Let us make the modern ploughshares—the computers—help people to prosper.   (Reuter News Service, 11/28/95)

What does the Bible say?

> And through his policy also he shall cause craft to prosper in his hand; and he shall magnify himself in his heart, and by peace shall destroy many: he shall also stand up against the Prince of princes; but he shall be broken without hand (Dan. 8:25).

Yasser Arafat, representative from the new Palestine state, addressed the Barcelona conference:

> He invited the twenty-six other participating nations to Bethlehem to join the Palestinians in four years' time in celebrating "one of the greatest events in human history, the second millennium of the birth of our Lord Jesus Christ, peace upon him. . . . On this occasion, I invite you to participate in this great world religious and historical event, and make Bethlehem a beacon of peace and coexistence of all faiths in the whole world, especially on the soil of Palestine, centre of three holy religions, Judaism, Christianity, and Islam. . . . Glory to God in heaven, peace on earth, and goodwill to all men," Arafat declared. (Reuter News Service, 11/28/95)

This sounds like reading one of old King Herod's speeches from Josephus—Herod, the cruel despot who killed all the children two years old and under in Bethlehem two thousand years ago. Herod was an Edomite, and now another Edomite, Arafat, is ruler over Bethlehem. The scenery on the world stage may have changed, but the actors are the same. The intermission between Daniel's sixty-ninth and seventieth prophetic week is about over.

Daniel 12:4 indicates that the increase of communications, travel, and knowledge would be signs that would indicate the nearness of the Kingdom Age with the coming of Messiah. Travel has increased almost miraculously in my generation. I learned to drive on a Model-T Ford with a top speed of about thirty miles an hour, but Adam could travel that fast on a horse in the Garden of Eden. Any part of the globe can now be reached by air travel from Oklahoma City within a twenty-four hour period. Jesus said of communications that we would see these things with our own two eyes, and this is certainly true today as any event in any part of the world can be seen within minutes over television. As far as knowledge is concerned, as reported by Prodigy, January 10, 1996, with the passage of Education Goals 2000 by Congress, academic standards (meaning without knowledge of God, Romans 1) will move our youth's minds to new heights of accomplishments.

World Party 2000

We read in Revelation 11 that the world will be rejoicing over the death of God's witnesses and sending each other gifts as time for the literal return of Jesus Christ winds down. The rich and famous have already reserved the most plush nightclubs and hotels in the world for a once-in-a-millennium celebration. A January 10, 1996, Prodigy news service item reports:

Starting to make plans for December 31, 1999? Forget it—you're probably already too late. . . . Although it's still four years off, the changing of the annual odometer to 2000 has already shaped up as the biggest blast of the twentieth century. Guest lists are filled in at some of the world's party hot spots. The Rainbow Room in Manhattan: there are 470 people ahead of you on the waiting list. The Savoy Hotel in London: the fortunate can enter a lottery for seats or rooms. Don't even try the Space Needle in Seattle: it's booked for a private party. Reservations are piling up for the annual Kaiser Ball in Vienna . . . at the posh La Tour d'Argent restaurant in Paris . . . at the Waldorf-Astoria in Manhattan. Looking for something more traditional? Colonial Williamsburg is full and there are 107 names on the waiting list. Good luck visiting Mickey or Minnie. Walt Disney World in Orlando, Florida, reports all seventeen company-owned inns are taken that night.

Other reports indicate that nightclub seats are going for $1,000 a couple, and a hotel suite for as high as $17,000 for one night. The world is planning for a big, big party to introduce the third millennium. What a time for the Rapture of the Church! The world would hardly miss us the next morning.

The Countdown

Are we saying that the Rapture of the Church and the Great Tribulation can be expected in the year 2000? Certainly not! We do say that the year A.D. 2000, a date of expectancy by the early Church, is a reasonable timetable, although the Rapture could occur at any time. That the end of the age is very near is evidenced by many signs which the prophets and Jesus gave:

1. Sign of the fig tree—Israel
2. Refounding of the Roman Empire

3. Comprehensive Middle East treaty in view
4. Jews getting ready to rebuild the Temple
5. Earthquakes increasing
6. Pandemic diseases like AIDS on the increase
7. Knowledge increasing
8. Communications explosion
9. New technologies making possible the mark of the Beast
10. New World Order
11. Storms and other warnings of nature
12. Days of Noah—increasing of crime and violence
13. Days of Lot—moral degeneracy and homosexuality
14. The world crying for peace, but there is no peace
15. Weapons of mass destruction
16. World wars and continuing wars
17. Space travel and signs in the heavens
18. Apostasy and the great falling away
19. The rise of false prophets and so-called world saviors
20. Communist revival in Russia and threats to move southward in a new imperialism
21. Arab fundamentalism and the rebuilding of Babylon
22. Jerusalem to be a burden to all people, and now surrounded on three sides by a new Palestinian army

Is it not exciting that Isaiah prophesied "in that day" the Great Pyramid would be a sign to the world? It is not coincidental that television programs about the mysteries of the Great Pyramid are increasingly telecast around the world. To even those nations that ban the Bible, the Great Pyramid is a prophecy in stone. The preceding list contains end-time signs outlined in the prophetic Word. Only those who are willfully ignorant can ignore evidence that the return of Jesus Christ is imminent, even at the door (2 Pet. 3). The countdown for Christ's return has already begun.

Chapter Nine

Prophetic Projections of the Pyramid

Prophets of God, Jeremiah and Isaiah, both referred to the Great Pyramid as one of the wonders of God in the midst of Egypt. Josephus indicated that in his day the Great Pyramid remained as a sign that God would one day destroy the world with fire. Therefore, we would assume that the Great Pyramid would have some eschatological significance. Some of the prophetic interpretations by men like David Davidson, Piazzi Smyth, George Riffert, and others may be worth our attention. Some pyramid-based projections are silly, nationalistic, and stupid. I am sure that God's eternal plan and purpose was not altered greatly when the Labor Party defeated the Tories in the British Parliament in 1902.

Nevertheless, the signs that Jesus referred to, both in Heaven and on Earth, are in evidence today. At the writing of this manuscript I am seventy-three years old. In my lifetime man has tried to cast away the cords of God and rush to build an empire reaching even to the heavens: radio, television, radar, computers, penicillin, antibiotics, unlocking the secrets of atoms, organ transplants, the information superhighway, space travel, etc.—all these things have come in my lifetime. We read in Daniel 9:26 that the end of this age would come as a flood. We are living in an age in which there is such a rush of man's accomplishments that the human is worshipped and the Divine is forgotten. Therefore, there are continuing increases in crime, divorce, drug usage, wars, terrorism, AIDS and other pandemic diseases, earthquakes, population, and environmental problems, a communist revival in Russia, rampaging Islamic expansion, international nuclear dispersion, etc., which are all the results of ignoring our Creator and depending on sinful, finite man for our deliverance and salvation.

Jesus said of the days before His Second Coming that men's hearts would be

> . . . failing them for fear, and for looking after those things which are coming on the earth . . . (Luke 21:26).

Paul wrote of the last days in 1 Thessalonians 5:2–3:

> For yourselves know perfectly that the day of the Lord so cometh as a thief in the night. For when they shall say, Peace and safety; then sudden destruction cometh upon them, as travail upon a woman with child; and they shall not escape.

In speaking of the unsaved and unregenerate masses, we notice that Paul used the pronoun "they" and not "we," in reference to the lost who will be left behind at the Rapture.

The hearts of men are looking with fear in anticipation of the future. Arnold Toynbee predicted a bleak future for the forces of freedom in his twelve-volume study of human history. He predicted an authoritarian and ruthless world government. Likewise, George Orwell, in his book *1984*, predicted a world dictatorship by that time, one in which everyone would become slaves to a world ruler.

The July 1, 1974, edition of *Time* magazine carried this suggestion:

> Kissinger's achievements have, at last, justified the establishment of

a new political office, which I sincerely hope the United Nations will consider: President of the Planet Earth.

Christians know that they have a Savior in times like these, but the unregenerate world is still searching for one. This is noted in the daily newspapers, and Jesus knew that the hopelessness of world conditions in the last days would impel many to such a messianic search. He prophesied this in Matthew 24:24: "For there shall arise false Christs, and false prophets. . . ."

In ages past, man did not have the written Word of God. Nevertheless, the Creator did not leave man in ignorance concerning His eternal will and purpose. Paul wrote in Romans 1:18–20 that God revealed to the ancients all the invisible things, even His righteous judgment, in things that are created, particularly the heavens. Dr. J. A. Seiss and E. W. Bullinger both have written monumental works on this revelation in the stars.

Balaam, according to all available evidence, received his knowledge of God and his prophetic insight from the stars, which revealed even the coming of a person of the Godhead who was to be born of woman. Balaam prophesied of this glorious event in Numbers 24:17:

> I shall see him, but not now: I shall behold him, but not nigh: there shall come a **Star** out of Jacob, and a Sceptre shall rise out of Israel. . . .

The wise men from the east who came looking for the newborn King of the Jews were also star prophets of the order of the Magi. It is ironic that the priests and Levites, who should have known from Daniel's prophecy of seventy weeks that it was time for the Messiah to be born, did not discern the signs of the times, although Gentiles from a far land, whose knowledge of God came only from the stars, were fully informed. There was absolutely no doubt in their minds as they spoke forthrightly to Herod:

> . . . Where is he that is born King of the Jews? for we have seen his star in the east, and are come to worship him (Matt. 2:2).

The relevance of all this to the Great Pyramid is that the knowledge of God's plan and purpose in the stars was also incorporated into the gigantic structure so that His detailed blueprint for the future was carved in stone.

For those interested in a thorough documentation of the mathematical and astronomical calculations incorporated into the Great Pyramid, we recommend David Davidson's book, *The Great Pyramid—Its Divine Message.* Although this book is out of print, one might be located in a bookstore that specializes in rare books that are no longer published.

In Matthew 23, Jesus prophesied that the generation to whom He spoke would see the destruction of Jerusalem and the Temple. It did. In Matthew 24, Jesus prophesied that the generation that witnessed the "beginning of sorrows," kingdom rising against kingdom, increase of earthquakes, Israel refounded as a nation, etc., would also see Him coming in power and great glory. Davidson and Aldersmith in their book, *The Great Pyramid—Its Divine Message,* considered the first step at the end of the Grand Gallery leading to the King's Chamber to represent the beginning of the time of sorrows that would precede Christ's return. They subsequently, by linear measurements, arrived at the following timetable for end-time events.

1909 (Face of Great Step) Leaders of Russia, France, and England met to consider dangers to world peace posed by rising German militarism.

1914 (Entrance doorway to Antechamber passage) World War I began.

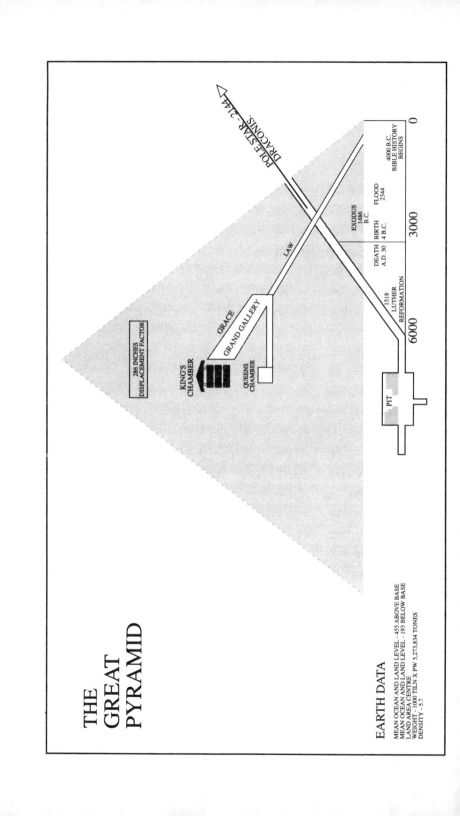

THE
GREAT
PYRAMID

POLE STAR - DRACONIS - 2144.

286 INCHES
DISPLACEMENT FACTOR

KING'S
CHAMBER

GRACE

GRAND GALLERY

QUEENS
CHAMBER

LAW

PIT

4000 B.C.
BIBLE HISTORY
BEGINS

0

FLOOD
2344

EXODUS
1486
B.C.

BIRTH
4 B.C.

3000

DEATH
A.D. 30

1518
LUTHER
REFORMATION

6000

EARTH DATA

MEAN OCEAN AND LAND LEVEL - 455 ABOVE BASE
MEAN OCEAN AND LAND LEVEL - 193 BELOW BASE
LAND AREA CENTRE
WEIGHT - 1000 TILLN X PW 5,273,834 TONES
DENSITY - 5.7

1918 (End of Antechamber passage) World War I ends.

1919 (Limestone ends, granite begins) Allies meet to consider international council to end war.

1924 (Center of granite floor in the Antechamber) A dating of the Great Pyramid's General Chronology System completed.

1926 (Halfway between Grand Gallery and King's Chamber) New phase of communist revolution in Russia declaring that nation to be against God; Chinese communists successful in securing northern provinces in China.

Following dates noted as being important, but not identified because book was published in 1927.

1936 (Low passage ends on threshold of King's Chamber) Gestapo given authority to kill all enemies of the state by Hitler; Jews excluded from protection of German law—beginning the extermination of 6 million Jews. The National Socialist Party (Nazi Party) announced to the world, "For modern society, a colossus with feet of clay, we shall create an unprecedented centralization which will unite all powers in the hands of government . . . which will mechanically govern all movements of individuals" (*Universal Standard Encyclopedia*, Vol. 16). Hitler's pronouncement identified the present world as being the feet of clay on the Gentile image (Dan. 2), but he did not become the Antichrist as planned.

1939 (Vertical line to south wall of Subterranean Chamber—time of trouble) World War II began, the most destructive war in terms of casualties and property in history.

1945 (South wall of King's Chamber) World War II ended.

Let us assume that those who have studied the Great Pyramid have concluded that the Grand Gallery does represent the offer of God's grace and salvation through faith in Jesus Christ to the entire world. It would naturally follow then, that the "Queen's Chamber" would represent the Church being created during the dispensation of grace, as foretold in Acts 15:14–16:

> Simeon hath declared how God at the first did visit the Gentiles, to take out of them a people for his name. **[This verse must refer to the Christian Church called out of all races, tongues, and nations.]** And to this agree the words of the prophets; as it is written. **[Although the Church is a mystery, nothing in the books of the prophets negates this mystery.]** After this . . . **[After what? After the Church has been completed and called out of this world at the Rapture.]** I will return . . . **[Jesus will not literally return to this Earth until after the Church has been called out to meet Him in the air, according to 1 Thess. 4:13–18.]** . . . and will build again the tabernacle of David, which is fallen down. . . .

The grand step at the end of the Grand Gallery could represent two things:

A. It could represent the flood of end-time events prophesied by Daniel and Jesus, which leads into the Antechamber. What does one do in a king's antechamber? He waits until the king summons him. The Church is in the last generation, waiting for the summons of the King: the Rapture.

B. The giant step could represent the Rapture at the end of the Church Age. This interpretation would therefore make the antechamber the place of judging of believers, the Judgment Seat of Christ before He, as King of kings, returns and brings the Church with Him to bring in His Kingdom on Earth.

On page 391 of *The Great Pyramid—Its Divine Message*, the authors made another interesting observation:

> The intersection of the Antechamber Symbolism into the natural period of Chaos reduces that period to 153 months of 30 days, defined by the sum of the lengths of the two Low Passages. The number 153 is the number of fishes in John 21:11.

While Drs. Davidson and Aldersmith were somewhat weak in their prophetic interpretation as to just what the number 153 has to do with the last days, they can certainly be complimented for even trying to make an application, especially in view of the fact that they wrote this seventy years ago.

In relating the prophetic significance of the number 153 to the last days, as revealed in the Great Pyramid, remember that Jesus said in Matthew 13:47–49:

> Again, the kingdom of heaven is like unto a net, that was cast into the sea, and gathered of every kind: Which, when it was full, they drew to shore, and sat down, and gathered the good into vessels, but cast the bad away. So shall it be at the end of the world. . . .

There are at least ten scriptures in the Old Testament which describe the bringing in of the nations into the Kingdom Age as a man gathering fish in a net. The good nations, those who accept Him as King of kings and Lord of lords, will be saved, but those who reject Him (Rev. 20: 7–9) will be destroyed. It seems apparent that the 153 fish of John 21:11 represent 153 nations on Earth when the Lord returns.

The Gentile image of world empires in Daniel 2 depicts a great breakup of such empires in the end of the age into smaller nations. Hitler did not mold the iron and clay in the feet of the image back together. Instead, after World War II, the great empires of England, Germany, France, Spain, Belgium, and Portugal, broke up into small nations. Whereas there were less than one hundred nations in 1945, today there are over one hundred and eighty. This breakup of Gentile empires is also prophesied in Luke 21:29–31:

> ... Behold the fig tree, and all the trees; When they now shoot forth, ye see and know of your own selves that summer is now nigh at hand. So likewise ye, when ye see these things come to pass, know ye that the kingdom of God is nigh at hand.

Date setting in any form is contrary to the exhortation given by Jesus in Matthew 24:36. Jesus did indeed say: "But of that day and hour knoweth no man, no, not the angels of heaven, but my Father only." Of course, it is a matter of interpretation whether Jesus was referring to the passing away of Heaven and Earth mentioned in the preceding verse, or His literal return as prophesied in the succeeding verse. In any event, it should be kept in mind that the gospel of Matthew is Jewish, and the Jews have been kept in spiritual darkness concerning not only the first advent, but the second advent as well. The words of Jesus in Matthew 24:36 have to be balanced against those of Luke 21:31:

> So likewise ye, when ye see these things come to pass, know ye that the
> kingdom of God is nigh at hand.

Luke's gospel is Gentile in orientation. From the prophecy of Daniel's seventy weeks, the Jews could have known the time of the birth of the Messiah. We read in Galatians 4:4 that Jesus was born in the "fulness of time," meaning a definite date in time. Yet, Scripture records that there were only two people in all Israel outside of Mary's immediate family who anticipated Christ's birth—an old priest by the name of Simeon and Anna the prophetess (Luke 2:25–38). The sin that brought on Israel's judgment was that of failing to discern the signs of the time and not knowing the time of their visitation (Luke 19:44).

It is obvious that anyone who becomes informed during the Tribulation—and the Bible indicates there will be millions—can know the time of Christ's return. Certainly, the 144,000 Jewish witnesses of God during the Tribulation will be spiritually awakened to the signs of the times. And those who are so enlightened will know that seven years from the time the Antichrist signs the covenant with Israel (Dan. 9:27), Christ will come. Anyone discerning the signs of the times when the Antichrist commits the Abomination of Desolation in the Temple will know it will be forty-two months to the day until Jesus Christ comes with all His angels (Rev. 13:5). The certainty of Christ's coming within a specified length of time will encourage millions to stand fast in their faith and refuse to take the mark of the Beast. While great numbers will become martyrs, many others will be saved out of all nations in order to repopulate the Earth (Zech. 14:16).

The fallacy of taking one scripture out of context has been proven over and over again. But it is *not* scriptural to present the evidence that God is working out His plan and purpose for the world according to a preordained schedule.

Jesus foretold in Matthew 24 that as the time for His return became imminent, false christs and false prophets would increase. One example of false christs is Louis Farrakhan, who in 1995 motivated one million black men (as he claimed) to mass in Washington D.C. under the umbrella of the Nation of Islam. Farrakhan claims that Jesus Christ was only a type of himself, that he himself is the real christ. False prophets through Christendom abound, claiming that they know the day and the hour Jesus Christ will return. However, Jesus did say that we could know when His return was near, even at the door. In 2 Peter 3:5, Peter said that Christians would have to be willingly ignorant not to know, in the last days, that the signs of the time indicated the Lord's return was at hand. The Lord's return should not keep us from faithfully discerning the signs of the times, including signs in the heavens.

The prophetic signs given to man in the Great Pyramid, including its prophetic calendar, are important because they parallel the fulfillment of prophecy in these last days as noted in the previous chapter. And what else besides the Great Pyramid could the prophet have referred to in Jeremiah 32:19-20?

> Great in counsel, and mighty in work: for thine eyes are open upon all the ways of the sons of men: to give every one according to his ways, and according to the fruit of his doings: Which hast set signs and wonders in the land of Egypt, even unto this day, and in Israel, and among other men; and hast made thee a name, as at this day.

Chapter Ten

Knowledge in the Ancient World

In this chapter we consider the mysterious scientific knowledge that appears to have been present in the ancient world.

The high degree of skills and accomplishments demonstrated in art, sculpture, architecture, carpentry, dress, masonry, and agriculture, evidences an even higher level of civilization in many areas than is present today. It was during this age before the flood that Josephus, and chronology, indicate that buildings and temples like the Great Pyramid were constructed. The fact that men lived to nine hundred years of age, remaining both physically and mentally active, would in itself indicate superior knowledge. *Fausset's Bible Dictionary* says of Methuselah:

> . . . he dies and it [the flood] is sent. A name given prophetically by Enoch—the longest lived, 969 years. He died in the year of the flood, or possibly in it.

Enoch was the father of Methuselah, and the name he gave his son proves that he knew the flood was coming. This would seem to be added evidence that Enoch could have been the builder of the Great Pyramid because, as we have already mentioned, Josephus wrote that the children of Seth built it to withstand the coming flood.

The theory of evolution proposes that the progress of man's knowledge paralleled his physical development that took place over millions of years. However, now even those who have held to this belief are being forced to admit that they may have been wrong. The Bible does not afford much insight into the degree of man's capabilities in the fields of arts and sciences before the flood. Nevertheless, we can with some measure of accuracy, read between the lines in the writing of Moses from the fourth chapter of Genesis:

> And Adah bare Jabal: he was the father of such as dwell in tents, and of such as have cattle (vs. 20).

It is evident that before the flood there were ranchers and farmers. For example, Cain was a farmer and Abel was a shepherd.

> And his brother's name was Jubal: he was the father of all such as handle the harp and organ (vs. 21).

Before the flood there were the knowledge, skills, and the means to make complicated instruments like the harp and the organ. The antediluvians also must have had the knowledge to compose, read, and play music.

> And Zillah, she also bare Tubal-cain, an instructor of every artificer in brass and iron . . . (vs. 22).

In the Antediluvian Age there must have been schools, because Tubal-cain was an instructor. From these schools there came musicians and artificers in metals. The dictionary defines an artificer as "a maker or craftsman, especially a skilled one . . . a person who devises; inventor." According to *Halley's Bible Handbook*, page 72, in pre-flood cities like Eridu, Obeid, Kish, Ur, and others, the citizens possessed painted pottery, hoes, mirrors, sickles, fish hooks, models of boats, pottery that was artistically painted with intricate geometric patterns, chariots, and the women used cosmetics. All of these indicate an astonishingly advanced civilization. Josephus wrote that the sons of Seth were schooled in the knowledge of astronomy.

In the year 1891, while excavating a tomb at Sakkara, Egypt, archaeologists found a birdlike object made of sycamore wood among the artifacts. They had no idea what it was as they had never seen an airplane, so they simply tagged it for identification purposes—the Sakkara bird. For years the object remained to observers simply a museum piece. Finally, after the invention and development of the airplane, it was noticed by aviation engineers as some kind of an advanced aircraft design. In the early seventies, it was examined by aeronautic engineers, who then concluded that the Sakkara bird was an exact model of a new, advanced, oblique-winged craft that NASA planned to build—the space shuttle *Challenger.* On page 53 of the September 1982 edition of *Omni,* the following observation about this Egyptian artifact, dating from 200 B.C., was made:

> And when the tiny wooden relic was subjected to the ultimate test—a flight trial—it soared through the air with the ease and grace of a modern day glider. To the experts, the conclusion was inescapable; the 2,000-year-old object was a model airplane. . . . The technical sophistication of age-old relics is so impressive that we have only recently come to understand their purposes, prompting some scholars to wonder: is it possible that the great scientific and technological achievements of the past five hundred years were already known to ancient civilizations?

Another item was discovered in 1936, southeast of Baghdad, Iraq: the item—a battery dating to 250 B.C.—demonstrates that man thousands of years ago possessed scientific knowledge and skills. The battery made from a clay pot shell contains an inner cylinder of copper with an iron rod core suspended in the center, indicating corrosive acid action that produced electricity. There were several of these batteries uncovered in the dig. Arne Eggebrecht of the Roemer Museum in Hildesheim, West Germany, in 1976 said:

> "To a scientist, they can only mean an electric cell." A replica of this ancient battery was made and filled with fresh grape juice, and it registered two volts of electricity. It appears certain that electricity was known and used two thousand years before its discovery was credited to Benjamin Franklin.

The question remains unanswered as to what use electricity was applied two thousand years ago—motors, lights, metal plating? The important thing for us to know today is that such knowledge and technical skills existed thousands of years before the so-called modern industrial and space ages.

In the year 1900 an unusual mechanism was discovered in a Greek merchant ship that had been sunk off the island of Antithera in 78 B.C. Because the item was very brittle and encased in a covering of limestone deposits, it was catalogued at Yale University as nothing more than a simple astrolabe. However, in 1971 it was studied through radiographs and discovered to be a complicated instrument having thirty gears—a planetarium that could chart the motions of the sun and the moon and determine their location in the past and where they would be in relation to the Earth in the future. Such complex instruments with differential gears did not appear in the West until 1575. Yet Ovid credited such an invention to Archimedes, the discoverer of the principle of gravity in 300 B.C.

Dr. Barry Fell, emeritus professor at Harvard, did extensive studies of artifacts relating to early settlers in America. He has written two books reporting his findings, and the evidence is substantiated with hundreds of actual photographs and charts. While it is generally accepted now that the Vikings established settlements along the East Coast of the United States and Canada five hundred years before Columbus discovered America, Dr. Fell has produced impressive evidence that North America was important to European and Middle Eastern cultures hundreds of years previous to the explorations of the Vikings. The following is a quotation from Dr. Fell's book, *Saga America:*

Over the span of fifteen centuries from 400 B.C. to A.D. 1100, the Western world was dominated by six maritime powers. In orderly succession, their fleets swept the Mediterranean and adjacent seas (Carthaginians, Greeks and Libyans, Romans, Byzantine Greeks, Islamic powers of North Africa). . . . These were not the only maritime peoples who visited our shores and sailed our great inland rivers and lakes. Others had come before: Celts, Iberians, and Basques from Spain, earlier Libyans, men of Egypt and Crete. . . . But after the fourth century B.C. our visitors began to bring with them—and to leave behind—the infallible date-markers that the modern historians demand: those enduring metal disks called coins . . . now being brought to light by the electronic metal detector. . . . The peoples of China and India found their way to our western shores. . . . The ancient Libyans . . . transcended all others in their spans of voyages. One of them, Eratosthenes of Cyrene, calculated the Earth's circumference, and then showed that if the ocean is continuous, one could sail around the Earth in either direction and return to the starting point. Libyans set out to test his theory. . . . Some of them established schools of learning here where mathematics, astronomy, navigation, and geography were taught as skills in the sciences. Ancient America, two thousand years ago, became a haven of refuge where learned men from Mediterranean lands imparted their knowledge to the young. . . . A golden age dawned . . . for centuries a breed of mariners set out from our shores to explore the Pacific and to trade with the peoples of Asia. Then, about a thousand years ago, that civilization began to crumble.

Photographically reproduced in Dr. Fell's books are the actual coins, weapons, pottery, and historical logs carved in stone in the visitor's language. On pages 280–81 of *Saga America*, the map of the world by Eratosthenes is reproduced—not in the shape of a plane rectangle, but a perfect globe, complete with latitudinal and longitudinal markings. By applying trigonometrical equations, he calculated the circumference of the Earth to be twenty-five thousand miles. Eratosthenes drew his map in 239 B.C. before he visited North America, 1,731 years before Columbus reportedly discovered America in 1492.

Recent archaeological discoveries also indicate that many of those who came to North America from Europe and North Africa in the first and second centuries were Christians and Jews who came to escape persecution. We quote from page 164 of *Saga America:*

> For over two thousand years America has served as a place of refuge for Old World communities driven from their homes by conquest or persecution. . . . It would appear to reflect a historic role of the New World through much of recorded history. A curious clay tablet found in a rock crevice near Big Bend, Texas, apparently tells us that Zoroastrians came once to America, seemingly from Iberia. . . . More striking are the evidences from Tennessee and Kentucky where the combined efforts have given us the outlines of an immigration there of homeless Jews after the several pogroms of Antiochus in Syria, and Nero and Hadrian in Rome. Evidently some Hebrews were already here in A.D 69 when the first revolt in Jerusalem against the Romans occurred. Josephus, who took part in the revolt, tells us that through the year A.D. 69 a great comet hung like a flaming sword over Jerusalem. The Zealots took it to be the sign of the coming of the promised Messiah. . . . Astronomers say that it was the regular

return of Halley's comet. A stone excavated from a burial mound in Tennessee at Bat Creek tells us that Jews in Tennessee recognized the sign and inscribed the stone "The Comet for the Jews"! Scattered Hebrew shekels dating from the second revolt in A.D. 132 occur in various parts of Kentucky and a nearby district of Arkansas.

Perhaps the most amazing evidence concerning the knowledge of ancient man is a map a Turkish naval officer gave the U.S. Navy Hydrographic Office in 1956. In 1979, Professor Charles H. Hapgood copyrighted his book, *Maps of the Ancient Sea Kings —Evidence of Advanced Civilization in the Ice Age*. This book entails a detailed study of this map, but for the sake of brevity, we quote from a report in the September 1982 edition of *Omni*:

Charles H. Hapgood, a professor of the history of science at Keene State College in New Hampshire, was one of the first experts to scrutinize the artifact. It was a fragment of a world map drawn on a gazelle hide in 1513 by Piri Re'is, an admiral in the Turkish navy. On one corner of the document, Re'is had written that the map had been compiled from some twenty-odd older maps, one of them drawn by Christopher Columbus. Ever since Columbus' historic voyages to America, historians have been searching for the legendary chart that guided him. Here, it seemed was evidence that such a map had once existed. One aspect of the Piri Re'is map especially caught Hapgood's attention: it seemed to chart correctly the coastline of Queen Maud Land in Antarctica—a feat modern science had not been able to accomplish until 1949 because of the thick ice sheet that covers the continent. Was the source map used by Piri Re'is drawn before the onslaught of the ice some 6,000 years ago? According to computer analysis, the original source map had been redrawn using plane trigonometry, prompting Hapgood to remark, "This was a total shock, since most experts believe that there was no trigonometrical foundation to the portolan charts." . . . The map correctly showed the contours of Antarctica before the ice sheet covered it. Hapgood's best estimate of when the original source map was drawn is 10,000 years ago. "The picture that seems to emerge, therefore," wrote Hapgood, "is of a scientific achievement far beyond the capabilities of the navigators and mapmakers of the Renaissance, or of the known geographers of ancient times." . . . Hapgood's findings have been accepted by the Cartographic Section of the U.S. Strategic Air Command and his methodology vouched for by the Rev. Daniel L. Linehan, director of Weston Observatory at Boston College, and by Professor Francis J. Heyden, director of the Georgetown University Observatory.

On page 58 of Professor Hapgood's book, he notes that the map shows a large island in the Atlantic Ocean between North Africa and the Americas. Some believe this extinct island was Atlantis, and the time element would correspond with Socrates' story that Atlantis sank in the ocean about ten thousand years ago. We take note from page 230 of *Maps of the Ancient Sea Kings:*

> It is becoming increasingly clear that something is drastically wrong with present theories regarding the antiquity of the Ice Age. It would seem to be a recent event. This is amply borne out by the maps.

On August 30, 1986, a news report given over Canadian television reported the discovery of a frozen forest only eight hundred miles from the North Pole. This was not petrified wood, but preserved trees with the roots of the stumps still imbedded in the soil. The wood could be sawed like normal wood. The tens and hundreds of millions of years of Earth's history proposed by the evolutionists can now seemingly be reduced to a few thousand years in accordance with biblical chronology. And it seems that the antediluvians had knowledge that has only recently been attained by modern man, and that they sailed the oceans from pole to pole.

Another interesting fact, brought out on page 231 of *Maps of the Ancient Sea Kings*, is about a people in the Mali Republic near Timbuktu called the Dogon who have linked their history to a star called Sirius that, from Earth, is invisible to the naked eye. We quote:

> It appears that the invisible companion of Sirius (now called Sirius B) has a very special importance to the Dogon, being central to their religious beliefs and rites. Their knowledge includes the fact that Sirius B travels in an elliptical orbit with Sirius as one of the foci of the ellipse. It seems that the Dogon also know the period of the revolution of Sirius B in its orbit, which is fifty years, and the fact that it rotates on its axis! Moreover, they know its relative density, calling it the heaviest thing in the universe. It is in fact a white dwarf star. The Dogon consider the moon to be dry and dead, that Saturn has a ring, that the planets revolve around the sun, and that the Milky Way is composed of distant stars. They know of four of the moons of Jupiter. They know of the circulation of blood and the existence of red and white blood corpuscles. They believe that Sirius is the star where the souls of dead go, and they believe space visitors were not human. . . . Robert Temple has traced the Dogon's traditions back to pre-dynastic Egypt. Perhaps we can trace them to the much older civilization that produced the map.

Where did these tribal people in Africa obtain this knowledge that has been passed down from generation to generation for over five thousand years? This puzzle, and many others, some of which we have noted, is one of the marginal mysteries of Scripture. We may also wonder why such knowledge was lost. The only answer we can suggest is given in Romans 1:21–22:

> Because that, when they knew God, they glorified him not as God, neither were thankful; but became vain in their imaginations, and

their foolish heart was darkened. Professing themselves to be wise, they became fools.

And we are told in Daniel 12:4 that in the time of the end "knowledge shall be increased." It would appear that modern man, like the ancients, are again making the same mistake.

Charles Darwin, the recognized father of the theory of evolution, attended Cambridge for three years in preparation for the ministry. Like many seminaries today, Cambridge turned out some students for the synagogue of Satan rather than equipping Christians for Christian service. On page 277, volume I, *Life and Letters*, Darwin wrote:

> For myself I do not believe that there ever was a revelation from God. As for a future life, every one must judge for himself between conflicting vague probabilities. . . . Then arises the doubt, can the mind of man which has, as I fully believe, been developed from the mind of the lowest animal, be trusted when it draws such grand conclusions?

In 1830 Darwin, after studying animal, bird, and marine life of the Galapagos Islands, continued on to the Fiji Islands in the South Pacific. In the Fiji Islands Darwin observed a wild, savage race of natives given to cannibalism. Thinking perhaps that the Fiji Islanders were still in a state of evolutionary development, young Darwin observed that these people were "hopelessly lost to civilization." Subsequently, missionaries from England brought the gospel of Jesus Christ to the islands and established mission stations and churches. In 1870 Charles Darwin visited the Fiji Islands once again, and reported:

> The march of improvement consequent upon the introduction of Christianity throughout the South Sea islands probably stands by

itself in the records of history. Within twenty years human sacrifices, the power of an idolatrous priesthood, profligacy unparalleled in any other part of the world, infanticide and bloody wars not sparing women and children, all these have been abolished; and dishonesty, intemperance and licentiousness have been greatly reduced (*Great Pyramid—Proof of God*, by George Riffert, p. 19).

There have been many reports of Charles Darwin renouncing his "theory of evolution" before he died in 1882, and again embracing salvation by faith in Jesus Christ. However, the preceding statement by Darwin is as close as we can document these reports. If there is further documentation, it is not in our research material.

When I was in the Fiji Islands, the fruits of the Christian missionaries who brought the story of redemption and salvation by God's only begotten Son, Jesus Christ, were still very much in evidence everywhere—much more so than among the aborigines of New Guinea. Nevertheless, by the acknowledged statement of the father of evolution himself, the elevation of man's spiritual and moral status can be attained instantly through a spiritual new birth in contrast to the so-called, imagined, "millions-of-years" evolutionary process.

Perhaps the greatest physical testimony constructed by man to the absurdity of the proposed "theory of evolution" which foolish man in his own wisdom has foisted upon the children of this generation is the Great Pyramid.

Chapter Eleven

The Sentinel of Time

The proof of the sixty-six books of the Bible to be the inspired Word of God lies in the intricate and almost unimaginable mathematical pattern of Scripture. We will not test the reader's patience by indulging in a lengthy presentation of the design of numbers like one, two, three, four, five, six, seven, eight, nine, ten, twenty, thirty, forty, fifty, etc. However, any number of books on biblical numerics prove that this mathematical pattern is found only in the Bible, and by considering that the Bible was written over a period of at least sixteen hundred years by at least forty writers, there is no way this numeric pattern could have been continued from book to book except the entire manuscript was dictated by an omniscient and omnipresent authority.

The Gentile Church Age is an inserted mystery of God into His dispensational timetable. Therefore, as the offer of the Kingdom was consistently refused by Israel on God's terms, numerics became less and less of eschatological importance. For example, we read that the disciples were to wait fifty days before assembling on the day of Pentecost. At the assembly there were one hundred and twenty brethren, and there was added unto them about three thousand souls. However, after Acts 4 no assembly is numbered, and no Church ministry is numbered other than meeting on the first day of the week.

As we enter the last days when Israel as a nation has been

refounded and the Kingdom is again in view, numbers once again become evident in transitional reverse.

1914 World War I begins

1917 England signs Balfour Declaration recognizing Israel's right to the land

1918 World War I ends

1918 Zionist Organization approves Balfour Declaration

1918 League of Nations is proposed to the world

1929 Great Depression

1939 World War II begins

1942 Holocaust

1945 World War II ends

1945 United Nations charter signed in San Francisco

1945 First atomic bomb used in war

1948 Breakup of Roman colonial system begins

1948 Israel refounded

1957 Six European nations unite as Common Market members at the Vatican

1967 Israel's Six Day War; Old Jerusalem back under Is-raeli control

1973 Yom Kippur War

1978 Camp David Agreement signed between Israel and Egypt

1988 Glasnost signaling the breakup of the USSR and Jews returning from the north

1991 Ethiopian Jews flown to Israel, completing return of the remnant

1992 Oslo Agreement between PLO and Israel

1992 Twelve members of the European Community sign European Union Declaration

God dealt with Israel in definite time periods, such as seven years, ten years, thirty years, forty years, fifty years, etc. When Israel again came into view in these latter years, God's prophetic clock began ticking once more.

Thirty years from the time the Jews received and verified the Balfour Declaration, Israel became a sovereign nation. Why thirty years? Because thirty is the Jewish age of maturity. No Jew could hold a political or ecclesiastical office until he reached the age of thirty. Jesus was thirty when He began His ministry. Sanhedrin members likewise had to be thirty.

Fifty years from the date the Gentiles (England) acknowledged the Jewish claim to Palestine, Jerusalem was taken from the Gentiles and restored to Israel. Again, why fifty years? Fifty is the Jewish year of Jubilee, or restoration. Every fiftieth year in Israel the land had to be restored to the heirs of the family who originally owned it, if a claim for restoration was made. Before the 1967 Six Day War, Israel had part of Jerusalem, but it was not the old Jerusalem with the Temple site recognized by God. This military miracle, and the restoration of Jerusalem, were prophesied twenty-five hundred years ago:

> In that day will I make the governors of Judah like an hearth of fire among the wood, and like a torch of fire in a sheaf; and they shall devour all the people round about, on the right hand and on the left: and Jerusalem shall be inhabited again **in her own place, even in Jerusalem** (Zech. 12:6).

While a local church building may be referred to in a spiritual sense as the Lord's House, only the Temple in Jerusalem can literally and scripturally be called by that name. It is so-called because the Temple floor is the place where the feet of the Messiah will stand as He appears to Israel in the Kingdom Age. The Temple will be the Lord's House. According to the prophecies, the Messiah cannot come until Israel builds Him a house (Ezek. 43:4-7; Mal. 3:1). When the Jews were permitted to return to Jerusalem after the Babylonian captivity, the first thing they did was build a Temple, but modern Israel has had the Temple site since 1967 and still there is no Temple, because the Dome of the Rock mosque remains where it has stood for the past thirteen hundred years. Israel cannot remove this Moslem shrine without risking a suicidal holy war that would involve the entire Arab world.

In presenting a futuristic chronology for Christ's return, keep in mind again these are only suggested dates that we may anticipate in light of present prophetic events. Concerning the restoration of the Jewish Temple, an important prophetic key that will unlock apocalyptic judgments, we refer to the *Jewish Chronicle* and the September 1984 edition of *Bible News Review* which both report plans to reconstruct the Tabernacle in the large paved space before the Wailing Wall, adjacent to the Temple site. Near this site is a special school, now training descendants of Levi and Aaron in Temple worship services. There are several prophetic scriptures, including Amos 9:11 and Acts 15:16, which indicate that the Tabernacle will be restored first, and then the Messiah will come and build the Millennial Temple. The word in Greek text for "temple" in 2 Thessalonians 2:4, and all other scriptures in reference to the Abomination of Desolation, actually means "holy place" and not a permanent structure.

The sixty-sixth chapter of Isaiah concerns the coming of Israel's Messiah to bring in the Kingdom with power and great glory (Isa. 66:15-18), but as the Lord appears over Jerusalem, He will ask, "Where is the house that ye build unto me? and where is the place of my rest?" (Isa. 66:1). This prophecy could also refer to the Tabernacle that will not be on the actual Temple site, prompting the question, "Where is the house that ye build unto me?" The actual House of the Lord will be built by the Messiah Himself when He comes (Zech. 6:12–13).

When we were last in Israel in November 1995, the yeshivas near the Western Wall were weaving priest's garments out of linen according to biblical specifications. Vessels for the Temple worship services were made, or are in the process of being made. Cohens and Levites were in training to resume sacrificial worship, and on a road between the Dead Sea and Eilat a sign announced the breeding of a "red heifer." The ashes of a pure and clean heifer with only red hair, not even one black or white hair, must be ready to cleanse the Temple and the vessels in order for the sacrifice and oblation to begin once more. All this must be ready for the King when He returns to set up His Kingdom on Earth, as represented by the empty coffer in the King's Chamber of the Great Pyramid.

Peter Tompkins, in his book *Secrets of the Great Pyramid*, points out the magnetic attraction which the Great Pyramid has held for would-be world rulers of all ages. Alexander the Great visited it while he was in Egypt. Afterward, the general went back through Jerusalem and thence to Babylon where he died. When Alexander was in Egypt he led a contingent of his army, after his visit to the Great Pyramid, to get his fortune told by a well-known seer at Silwan in the Libyan Desert. Whatever the mystic told Alexander, it must have made a great impression on him because he left instructions that after his death his body was to be buried at Silwan. In 1995, an elaborate Grecian-style crypt was discovered at Silwan. Also, ancient scripts were located which indicated that Alexander's generals did see to it that his body was interred at Silwan, approximately twelve hundred miles from where he died in Babylon.

On May 19, 1798, General Napoleon Bonaparte departed from France for Egypt with an army of thirty-five thousand men in a fleet of three hundred and twenty-eight ships. His object was first to conquer Egypt, then march eastward all the way to India, and so attain world domination. Just two months later, on July 12, 1798, while camping in the shadow of the Great Pyramid of Giza, the French were attacked by an Egyptian force estimated at seventy-eight thousand infantryman and cavalry. An overwhelming victory by the French resulted, with one report indicating that only forty of Napoleon's soldiers were killed. The bodies of the Egyptians, after being looted of gold and jewels, were cast into the Nile to float to the sea bearing news of the disastrous defeat and casting fear into the hearts of all the inhabitants and rulers of the land.

Tompkins gives this account of what happened when Napoleon visited the inside of the Great Pyramid:

> On the twenty-fifth of Termidor (revolution date for August 12, 1798), the General-in-Chief visited the Pyramid with Iman Nuhammed as his guide; at a certain point Bonaparte asked to be left alone in the King's Chamber, as Alexander the Great was reported to have done before him. Coming out, the general is said to have been very pale and impressed. When an aide asked him in a jocular tone if he had witnessed anything mysterious, Bonaparte replied abruptly that he had no comment, adding in a gentler voice that he never wanted the incident mentioned again. Many years later, when he was emperor, Napoleon continued to refuse to speak of this strange occurrence in the Pyramid, merely hinting that he had received some presage of his destiny. At St. Helena, just before the end, he seems to have been on the point of confiding to Las Cases, but instead he shook his head, saying, "No, what's the use. You'd never believe me."

After his tremendous victory over the Marmalukes of Egypt, Napoleon ordered his troops back on the ships and sailed eastward. Although Napoleon was not a loyal subject of the pope, he seemed to be an avid Bible reader, and he was intrigued with biblical prophecy. Napoleon's ships anchored in what now is the Jaffa Harbor. It appears the general intended to bypass Jerusalem and deal with the Turks in northern Israel. Jerusalem was well defended and Sulemein the Great had built a strong defensive wall around the city. Napoleon did not want to be attacked from the rear. All would-be world conquerors desire Jerusalem because Satan knows it is to be the capitol of God's Millennial Kingdom. Even when Hitler was embroiled in a life and death struggle with England and Russia, he still sent a double pincer toward Jerusalem. One army advanced through the Balkans with Turkey as an ally, while the second army advanced eastward across North Africa. He never quite reached Jerusalem.

From the Jaffa Harbor Napoleon took part of his army and traveled approximately fifteen miles eastward past Mt. Carmel to Mt. Megiddo. Besides being the prophetic marshaling point for the armies engaged in the coming battle of Armageddon, it has always been an important fort to control passage through the Valley of Jezreel. *Halley's Bible Handbook* and other historical sources aver that more blood has been shed at Megiddo than any other place on Earth. It seems logical that Napoleon wanted to secure Megiddo before marching up the coast to attack the Turkish stronghold at Acre. A multitude of historical notes quote Napoleon as saying, while standing on Mt. Megiddo and surveying the flat Jezreel Valley from Mt. Carmel to the Sea of Galilee, that all the armies of the world could maneuver on these plains. Each time I stand on Mt. Megiddo I remember the words of Napoleon, which he probably spoke because he did study prophecy and he knew from the book of Revelation that this would one day occur. Perhaps he thought this would happen at that time, and that he would be the great commander of the army of God.

The stronghold at Acre was built by the Crusaders in about A.D. 1100. The Crusaders were tremendous builders. They built impressive and impregnable castles. When the Arab's attacked, they would simply go back into their castles and wait until their enemies ran out of food. Boufort Castle was just to the north of Napoleon. I have been near Boufort Castle. A radio station that carried our program was near this PLO stronghold. After I was there, a Muslim force swept down and killed all the station attendants. I have also been to Kraak, the largest of the Crusader castles in Lebanon, and also visited what I consider one of the seven wonders of the world, the Castle of the Knights, built by Richard the Lionhearted, on a mountain on the east side of the Baka Valley near Damascus.

When a castle, of necessity, had to be built on a plain, the Crusaders encircled it with a well-built double moat defensive network. Thinking that he could gain a quick and easy victory like he attained at Cairo, Napoleon ordered a charge against the castle walls. The bodies of his soldiers filled up the first moat, but before the fallen soldiers filled up the second moat, Napoleon began to run out of men. Some historical notes indicate that of his thirty-five thousand-man army, only a little more than eight thousand were left after the Battle of Acre. The remainder of his army, with a much wiser Napoleon, boarded the ships anchored in the harbor and sailed back to France. This was one of Napoleon's most humiliating defeats. He was a brilliant strategist, but at times he was much too stubborn to order a strategic withdrawal. This fallacy probably caused his defeat at Waterloo.

Did Napoleon really receive a revelation from God while standing in the Great Pyramid? While this may be debated, we do know that Napoleon seemed resigned to the outcome of the Battle of Waterloo even before it began, and his final defeat in this battle has often been regarded as an act of God. Napoleon was a would-be world ruler who lived before his time, because the preordained time for the final Gentile ruler of Earth had not arrived. The great general himself seemed to realize this, and he realized also that Jesus Christ was God's anointed King of kings, as reflected in his dissertations during his last days on St. Helena. *Halley's Bible Handbook* reports Napoleon as saying:

> Alexander, Caesar, Charlemagne, and myself founded empires; but upon what? Force. Jesus founded his empire on Love; and at this hour millions would die for him. I myself have inspired multitudes with such affection that they would die for me. But my presence was necessary. Now that I am in St. Helena, where are my friends? I am forgotten, soon to return to the earth, and become food for worms. What an abyss between my misery and the eternal kingdom of Christ, who is proclaimed, loved, adored, and which is extending over all the earth. Is this death? I tell you, the death of Christ is the death of a God. I tell you, **Jesus Christ is God** (emphasis added).

These words of Napoleon reflect the message of the Great Pyramid. It has been encompassed by world conquerors, plundered by would-be thieves and robbers, denuded of its twenty-two acres of shining marble covering, and today it is examined by scientists with computers, radar, and other types of scientific equipment in an effort to unlock its ageless secrets. Yet, the Great Pyramid, the only remaining wonder of the ancient world, still stands like an eternal sentinel of time that spans the gap from the beginning to the end. It has declared its message, not only to kings and conquerors, but also to the world today. As Josephus wrote, it bears testimony that a second judgment, a judgment by fire, is coming upon the Earth because of the wickedness of men. This message in stone is also declared in the written Word:

. . . the Lord Jesus shall be revealed from heaven with his mighty angels, In flaming fire taking vengeance on them that know not God, and that obey not the gospel of our Lord Jesus Christ (2 Thess. 1:7–8).

Chapter 12

The Pyramid and the New Jerusalem

We read in Hebrews 9:21–24 that the Tabernacle, the altars, and the holy vessels were patterns or figures of the real Tabernacle and things of God in Heaven. We are not specifically informed about this in the Old Testament. Paul said that he was caught up to the third Heaven, which is God's Heaven, and he saw things which he could not describe. However, it is apparent that he saw enough to understand that the things of God in Heaven are revealed in type here on Earth.

We know that certain things in Heaven were revealed in type to Moses, and other heavenly scenes were revealed in the same way to Ezekiel, Daniel, and other prophets. But before Moses there was Abraham, the federal head of the Hebrew race and the father in faith of all who believe on Jesus Christ as Lord and Savior, and we know from the Bible that God also revealed something to him. It was so wonderful and so marvelous that he left his shepherd kingdom and set out across the wilderness in order to get just a glimpse of it. We read in Hebrews 11:8–10:

> By faith Abraham, when he was called to go out into a place which he should after receive for an inheritance, obeyed; and he went out, not knowing whither he went. By faith he sojourned in the land of promise, as in a strange country, dwelling in tabernacles with Isaac and Jacob, the heirs with him of the same promise: For he looked for a city which hath foundations, whose builder and maker is God.

It is not mere speculation to conclude that God showed Abraham a figure of the New Jerusalem in the same manner that He revealed to Moses an outline of the Temple in Heaven through the blueprint of the Tabernacle that He gave the children of Israel. It is recorded in ancient Egyptian hieroglyphics that the king who reigned about the year 2000 B.C. received a delegation of Shemite visitors from the east. This was approximately the time when Abraham traveled westward from the land of Canaan to the Nile. And according to Erick Von Daniken in his book, *Chariots of the Gods*, the summer palace of the kings of Egypt was only a short distance from the Great Pyramid. We must remember that Abraham was of royal blood himself, a shepherd king with much power and an extensive dominion. Abraham's army destroyed the combined armies of several Syrian kings (Heb. 7:1–3; Gen. 14). It would be unthinkable that the king of Egypt would not receive such a royal personage, and the patriarch could well be the Shemite mentioned in Egyptian history. If this is so, Abraham would have seen the Great Pyramid. Notice again the wording of Hebrews 11:10: ". . . he looked for a city which hath foundations, whose builder and maker is God."

Fausset's Bible Dictionary gives the following meaning for Jerusalem: "JERU—The foundation, implying its divinely given stability. SALEM—peace."

It is agreed by architects and archaeologists who have studied the Great Pyramid that it has the most solid foundation to be found in any structure on Earth. After more than four thousand years, in spite of its immense weight, it has not settled so much as a fraction of an inch. Von Daniken continues:

> The Great Pyramid is visible testimony of a technique that has never been understood. Today, in the twentieth century, no architect could build a copy of the pyramid of Cheops, even if the technical resources of every continent were at his disposal.

This observation has caused some to conclude that the builders must have had extraterrestrial, and possibly Divine, assistance.

It has been noted in reports of visitors to ancient Egypt, who saw the Great Pyramid while it still had its glistening outer cover of finely polished white limestone, that from a distance it looked like a magnificent vision descending from the sky. Clarence Larkin (referencing Herodotus) said of it:

> The Great Pyramid, as originally constructed, was built of granite overlaid with white limestone, and its exterior surface was smooth and unmountable, and it appeared like a building let down from Heaven.

We read of the New Jerusalem, the city after which Abraham sought:

> And I John saw the holy city, new Jerusalem, coming down from God out of heaven, prepared as a bride adorned for her husband. And I heard a great voice out of heaven saying, Behold, the tabernacle of God is with men, and he will dwell with them, and they shall be his people, and God himself shall be with them, and be their God (Rev. 21:2–3).

The location of the Throne Room in the Great Pyramid in relation to the Queen's Chamber also carries out the design given for the New Jerusalem. We read in Revelation 21:23: "And the city had no need of the sun, neither of the moon, to shine in it: for the glory of God did lighten it, and the Lamb is the light thereof." We continue in chapter 22, verse 17: "And the Spirit and the bride say, Come. And let him that heareth say, Come. And let him that is athirst come. And whosoever will, let him take the water of life freely."

The shaft leading downward in the Great Pyramid, also called the well, is just off the hallway leading to the Queen's Chamber.

The prophets of Israel were concerned with one main question about the ages to come: When would God fulfill the covenants to the fathers and bring the Kingdom of Heaven to Earth? It was in answer to Daniel's beseeching prayer concerning the advent of the Kingdom that God gave him the prophetic vision of the seventy weeks. The one question that the apostles asked Jesus over and over was, "Lord, wilt thou at this time bring in the kingdom?" Therefore, the Great Pyramid as a figure of the New Jerusalem should certainly contain a prophecy relating to the consummation of the ages.

In the 1920s and '30s, many students of prophecy began to draw prophetic charts and convert measurements of distance within the Great Pyramid to years in an attempt to foretell the exact date of the Rapture of the Church, the Tribulation period, and the Second Coming of Jesus Christ. We will not comment on all of these methods of prophetic computation, but we will mention one of the more common methods, converting inches to years.

It was discovered that a line drawn from a slab of granite in the Antechamber, down through the base of the Grand Gallery to a point intersecting an imaginary extended line from the side of the pyramid, was six thousand inches long. Assuming the creation of man in 4000 B.C. to be represented by that intersection, it was a relatively simple matter to pinpoint the birth of Christ about thirty inches down from the hall leading to the Queen's Chamber, where it widens out into the Grand Gallery. World War I was easily established as occurring at the beginning of the opening leading to the Antechamber. The end of that war in 1918 occurred where the line emerged from the opening into the Antechamber. From this point on into the King's Chamber, others have, at various points, attempted to set the date for the Rapture of the Church and the Second Coming of Christ. When the Church was not raptured and Christ did not come again, teachings on the Great Pyramid rapidly fell into disrepute, and many began to say there was no spiritual significance or biblical truth at all concealed within the pyramid's construction.

This only proved the fallacy of irresponsible date-setting. We firmly believe the entrance of the King's Antechamber does signify the beginning of World War I, and that this was the beginning of the time of the end referred to by Jesus in the Olivet Discourse. We ask again, against the obvious, what does a subject do in a king's antechamber? He waits for the king to summon him. The last generation of this age is waiting for a summons in the King's Antechamber. The Church will be summoned into the presence of the King, and the ungodly will be left outside to go through the judgments of the Tribulation. We read the summons to the Church in 1 Thessalonians 4:16–17:

> For the Lord himself shall descend from heaven with a shout, with the voice of the archangel, and with the trump of God: and the dead in Christ shall rise first: Then we which are alive and remain shall be caught up together with them in the clouds, to meet the Lord in the air: and so shall we ever be with the Lord.

But of the ungodly, those who are in rebellion against the King, we read in 1 Thessalonians 5:3:

> For when they shall say, Peace and safety; then sudden destruction cometh upon them, as travail upon a woman with child; and they shall not escape.

While the inside of the Great Pyramid is designed prophetically on a six thousand-year period of history from the creation of the first Adam to the appearance of the last Adam, Jesus Christ, the heavenly design is predicated upon a much greater length of

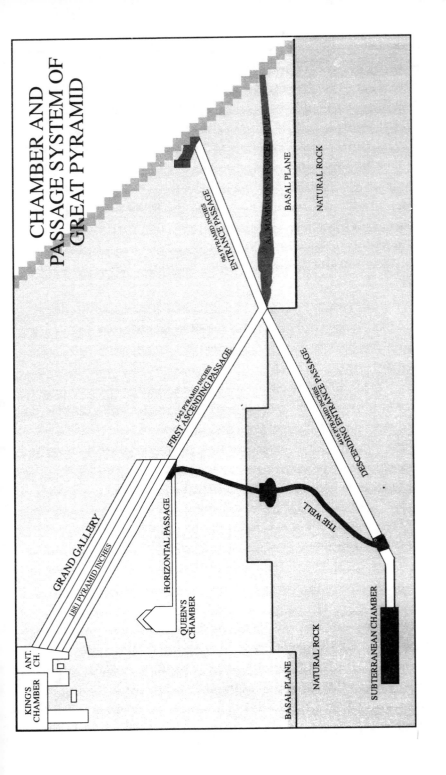

CHAMBER AND PASSAGE SYSTEM OF GREAT PYRAMID

KING'S CHAMBER

ANT. CH.

GRAND GALLERY

1881 PYRAMID INCHES

FIRST ASCENDING PASSAGE

1542 PYRAMID INCHES

HORIZONTAL PASSAGE

QUEEN'S CHAMBER

985 PYRAMID INCHES ENTRANCE PASSAGE

AL MAMOON'S FORCED PASSAGE

BASAL PLANE

NATURAL ROCK

4416 PYRAMID INCHES DESCENDING ENTRANCE PASSAGE

THE WELL

BASAL PLANE

NATURAL ROCK

SUBTERRANEAN CHAMBER

time. This extended period of time is also revealed in the construction of the Sphinx, which stands like a giant guardian over the pyramids until the entire course of time has expired.

The sum of the diagonals of the base of the Great Pyramid totals 25,826.54 inches, and it will require 25,826 years for the sun to make its journey through the twelve signs of the zodiac. The completed circuit is known as the precession of the equinoxes. This basic fact of astronomy was not only included in the dimensions of the Great Pyramid, but was also embodied within the design of the Sphinx. Quoting from the *Companion Bible:*

> The one great central truth of all prophecy is—the coming of One, Who, though He should suffer, would in the end crush the head of the old serpent, the Devil. But, where are we to open this book? Where are we to break into this circle of the zodiacal signs? Through the precession of the equinoxes, the sun gradually shifts its position a little each year, till in about every 2,000 years it begins the year in a different sign. This was foreseen; and it was also foreseen that succeeding generations would not know when and where the sun began its course, and where the teachings of this heavenly Book commenced, and where we were to open its first page. Hence the "Sphinx" was invented as a memorial. It had the head of a woman and the body and tail of a lion, to tell us that this Book, written in the heavens, began with the sign "Virgo" and will end with the sign "Leo." The word "sphinx" is from the Greek "sphingo," to join; because it binds together the two ends of this circle in the heavens.

As we have already stated, all authoritative Bible chronologies indicate a six thousand-year history for man, dating from the creation of the first Adam to the final dominion of the last Adam. If we add to this period of time one thousand years for the Millennium, we still have a total time period of only seven thousand years. This falls short of the over 25,000-year period required for the precession of the equinoxes. Where do the extra eighteen thousand years-plus come into view?

We read in Genesis 1:1–2:

> In the beginning God created the heaven and the earth. And the earth was without form, and void; and darkness was upon the face of the deep. And the Spirit of God moved upon the face of the waters.

The Hebrew text indicates that the Earth became without form and void because of a prior judgment, and we can only conclude that this judgment was caused by the rebellion of Lucifer, who fell from his exalted position and became Satan, but no one knows how long the Earth was under water. There is also a possible time gap between Revelation 20 and Revelation 21, when the Great White Throne Judgment is set and the first Heaven and the first Earth pass away. In any event, E. W. Bullinger and several other Bible scholars believe that the precession of the equinoxes is God's timepiece in the zodiac, just as there are twelve figures on our clocks and watches, and when the sun completes its run through the last sign this Earth will pass away and there will be a new Earth in accordance with Revelation 21. However, this is in no way an endorsement of astrology, which is an apostate science and a departure from the true science of astronomy that God revealed to the sons of Seth. Neither do we subscribe to theistic evolution which makes the days of creation into thousand-year days, or ages of a million or billion years each. Neither do we promote the time-gap theory between Genesis 1:1 and Genesis 1:2.

In considering the Great Pyramid as a type of the New Jerusalem, we present the following parallels:

a. The Great Pyramid is said to be the most perfect building possible as far as human abilities extend.

b. It has a sure foundation, a solid foundation of deep rock that has sustained the heaviest weight of any building constructed, without moving an inch in approximately five thousand years.

c. The six thousand-inch base line projects six thousand years for man's day and looks forward to the Millennium, the Lord's Day.

d. The empty coffer in the King's Chamber signifies that Jesus Christ, who died and was buried, has risen, that He is alive, and He will return as King of kings.

e. The Queen's Chamber refers to a mansion in the New Jerusalem reserved for the Church.

f. The 144,000 missing limestone casing blocks refer to the 144,000 Jewish evangelists who will be God's witnesses on Earth during the Great Tribulation. Their reward will be a special one. They will be taken up into Heaven, into the New Jerusalem, and be in the Holy City when it descends upon the Earth (Rev. 14:1–5).

g. The millions of stones in the Great Pyramid refer to the redeemed of all ages, or the lively stones of God's completed house (2 Pet. 4:1–5).

h. The missing cornerstone refers to Jesus Christ, the Head Cornerstone, who will be the capstone of the New Jerusalem (2 Pet. 2:6–8).

i. The pit, representative of Hades, is not part of the Great Pyramid. It is directly below the King's Chamber. The pit is equal in distance below the first masonry level as the King's Chamber is above the first level. Everyone in the world today is either on their way to see the King, or on their way to Hell. "And death and hell were cast into the lake of fire. This is the second death. And whosoever was not found written in the book of life was cast into the lake of fire" (Rev. 20:14–15).

Ten things about the New Jerusalem:

1. It is called the Holy City because nothing unclean or unholy will ever enter its gates (Rev. 21:2; 22:19).
2. It is called "new" because it will never grow old. It will never need an urban renewal project (Rev. 1:2; Heb. 11:10–16).
3. It is called the "tabernacle of God" because it is the dwelling place of God, and the shepherd takes his tent, or tabernacle, with him (Rev. 21:3).
4. It is called the Bride, the Lamb's wife, because it will be the eternal home of the Church (Rev. 19:7–10, 21:2; Eph. 5:23).
5. It is called the Heavenly Jerusalem because it is now in Heaven, and it will come down to Earth from Heaven (Rev. 21:2; Heb. 12:22).
6. It is called the Father's House because God built it for His own family (John 14:1–3).
7. It has twelve gates and twelve foundations. Twelve is the number of perfect government—there will be a perfect King and perfect justice—no more elections, no more jails (Rev. 21:12).
8. No sun, no moon, perfect temperature—God will light the city with His glory (Rev. 22:5).
9. The New Jerusalem is fifteen hundred miles square with streets of gold, and the entire city is adorned with diamonds, pearls, and all other kinds of precious gems (Rev. 21:16–21).
10. There will be no sinners in the New Jerusalem; in-

habitants will do the will of God at all times; all sorrow, sickness, and death will be abolished (Rev. 21:4; 1 Cor. 15:24–28).

The New Jerusalem is now, and will be forever, the capitol of the universe. However, we read in Ephesians 3:8–12 that we will boldly rule the heavenly places. Each Christian may have his own planet.

We read of the New Jerusalem as the eternal home of the saved of all ages in Hebrews 12:22–24:

But ye are come unto mount Sion, and unto the city of the living God, the heavenly Jerusalem, and to an innumerable company of angels, To the general assembly and church of the firstborn, which are written in heaven, and to God the Judge of all, and to the spirits of just men made perfect, And to Jesus the mediator of the new covenant, and to the blood of sprinkling, that speaketh better things than that of Abel.

Chapter Thirteen

Pyramid Phenomena and Angelic Visitors

The prophet Daniel noted that one of the signs of the last days would be a great increase of knowledge (Dan. 12:4). Man's secular knowledge today is, according to some educators, doubling every two and one-half years. As part of this increase of knowledge, scientists are learning that many of the stone relics of the past, including the Great Pyramid, were more than simply monuments to appease the vanity of men. Other theories are being postulated about the Great Pyramid and the ring of pyramid-shaped buildings which appear to circle the Earth at the equator. In considering a possible added purpose for the construction of the pyramid, we quote from *Did Genesis Man Conquer Space?* by Dr. Emil Gaverluk and Jack Hamm:

> Walter G. Dimmick of Sunnyvale, California, an electronics engineer, theorizes that the great pyramids of Egypt were giant radio transmitters and receivers. The top part of the pyramid would be a radio energy feed horn. . . . Today we build antennas in the pyramidal shape. . . . The size of Cheops pyramid would determine its power. . . . Dimmick says that if he is right in assuming that this is a huge radio transmitter pointing into space, then it is the second largest radio transmitter the world has ever seen.

Recent archaeological investigations into the pyramid-shaped temples in South and Central America have revealed that many of them may have been observatories. We know that their builders had a calendar that was more accurate than ours today.

Modern computers have determined that Stonehenge in England may have been used as a gigantic astronomical instrument. In their book *The Great Pyramid—Its Divine Message*, D. Davidson and H. Aldersmith offer substantial evidence that the same principles of mathematics and system of measurements were used in the construction of Stonehenge as were used in building the Great Pyramid:

> The evidence of archaeology, folklore, and tradition—together with the astronomical alignments and datings—has established the Eastern origin of the builders of Stonehenge. The evidence has shown that the two astronomical ideas of the British megalithic builders had been formulated in ancient Egypt. From Professor Petrie's data we find that the Stonehenge Circle is a constructional expression of the geometrical relations holding between the ancient Egyptian square and the linear systems of measures. . . . The outer ring of stones is the exact area of an important Egyptian unit of square measure.

Silbury Hill in Wiltshire, England, is pyramidal in shape and covers five acres. It still contains over a million tons of hand-moved material, even after thousands of years of erosion. According to *Secrets of the Great Pyramid* by Tompkins, archaeologists say it was constructed at least four thousand years ago, possibly before the flood. We could cite many more examples of advanced scientific and astronomical knowledge before the flood and also show evidence of the common mathematical equations used in the construction of many ancient pyramid-shaped temples and monuments, but such information would become repetitious. Those interested in pursuing the matter will find a number of books on the subject.

It was the correlation of such archaeological evidence that produced *Chariots of the Gods* by Erick Von Daniken. In conjunction with modern UFO sightings, Von Daniken theorizes that inasmuch as all religions are based upon the worship of a god or gods who live in the heavens, they all sprang from a central and common source—extraterrestrial beings who visited the Earth from other planets and who represented civilizations thousands or millions of years ahead of our own. Even judgment for sin is explained by Von Daniken in this way:

> . . . The "gods" were interested in passing on their intelligence. They took care of the creatures they bred: they wanted to protect them from corruption and preserve them from evil. They wanted to ensure that their community developed constructively. They wiped out the freaks and saw to it that the remainder received the basic requirements for a society capable of development.

After reading *Chariots of the Gods*, one dear saint wrote us: "I would give anything I owned if I had never read this book. Von Daniken has robbed me of my precious faith and left me with nothing but doubts about the future."

Christians who are bothered by the theories of Von Daniken should remember that they are theories only. The author himself says: "Admittedly this speculation is still full of holes. This book puts forward a hypothesis made up of many speculations."

If Earth has been and is being visited by astronauts from another solar system, who created them? Who created their world? All Von Daniken has actually done is to present reasonable evidence that Earth has been, and possibly still is, under observation by a superior life form. The fact remains that the entire universe, and all things therein, reveal a central intelligence, a supreme Creator, Designer, and Sustainer. This Creator is God, and above Him or below Him there is no other god.

We would agree with Von Daniken that the Earth has been visited by beings from outer space for thousands of years. The man who doubtless examined more evidence of extraterrestrial visitations than any other was Dr. J. Allen Hynek (director of Lindeheimer Astronomical Research Center at Northwestern University; associate director of the Smithsonian Astrophysical Observatory; a consultant to NASA; and for twenty years a consultant on UFO investigation of the U.S. Air Force). Dr. Hynek said:

> I cannot presume to describe what UFOs are because I don't know; but I can establish beyond reasonable doubt that they are not all misconceptions or hoaxes.

The Bible records an almost unlimited number of angelic excursions to the Earth. God's Kingdom is a celestial government. The guardians of the Temple of Heaven and the secret places of the Most High are the cherubim; the heavenly priests who direct worship to the Creator are the seraphim (Gen. 3:24; Kings 6:32; Isa. 6:2,6). The angels, which are innumerable, are messengers of God, as their name in the Greek indicates. The archangels are the provincial rulers over the angels. God has also set four watchers over the whole creation, and He has convened a heavenly senate of twenty-four members who govern in delegated authority (Dan. 4:17; Rev. 4:2-7). There can be no throne or kingdom without laws, subjects, judicial, legislative, and executive agencies.

I know of no one who has personally examined an angel. Several who say they had personal knowledge of either one or two UFOs that reportedly crashed in New Mexico have stated without qualification that the Air Force took from two to four alien bodies from the crash scene, and that these bodies are still in cold storage. We do not say this is true, or not true. These witnesses do appear to be honest, credible people and they still appear from time to time on television documentaries.

Recently a gentleman who is prominent in producing documentaries for television and the movie industry gave me a list of five hundred names of scientists, NASA personnel (including astronauts), airline pilots (both military and domestic), and prominent personalities, who had personally seen objects in the sky that they could not explain. When I mentioned to a scientist friend of mine that I was considering contacting some of these people on the list for a possible radio program series, he discouraged me from doing so. He indicated that this might put me in the kook-fringe crowd and discredit our entire ministry. Perhaps he is right; however, I personally know, without any doubt, that there are alien spacecraft in our skies.

In the summer of 1937, when I was fifteen years old, I saw three flying objects in the sky that I have never been able to explain. At that time I lived on a farm three miles southeast of Hugo in southeast Oklahoma. The time was about fifteen minutes after the sun had set in the west. As I was walking through the pasture to my home, there suddenly shot up in the sky from over the horizon in the east, a ball of light. From the distance it came, it appeared about the size of a chicken egg. The action would have been comparable to that of Roman candle fireworks, but at about twice the speed. It stopped suddenly in the sky over me without any slowing or braking motion whatsoever. It was difficult for me to accept what I saw. Then, on the same trajectory, there came another ball of light and stopped with the same motion just to the east of the first one, and it was followed by a third at about another ten second interval. All three balls of light, slightly pulsating from hues of white, yellow, and blue, just hung in the sky motionless. I had never heard of such things as UFOs at that time, and in 1935 there were not even helicopters. Later, in World War II, I served as a radar operator for a 90M antiaircraft battalion, but I never picked anything up on radar that I could not explain. The objects I saw in 1935 did not move for an hour, so I went into my home for dinner. After eating, I came out to see if they were still in the sky but they had evidently gone. There is nothing that I am aware of ever made by human hands (past, present, or planned) that could maneuver like the balls of light that I saw. They were evidently controlled by a superior intelligence, yet in no way could a human being have been present in one of those objects and lived.

There are thousands of reports on record similar to mine regarding UFOs. I have two personal friends who live in the Peoria, Illinois, area. They are an outstanding, honest, and hardworking Christian couple who have been married for thirty-five years. Both present, they related to me an experience with a UFO. Returning to their farm from Peoria at night, they were followed by a UFO on their country road. Finally, the husband stopped his car as the UFO hovered in front of them. As the husband got out of the car, his wife almost clawed his clothes off to keep him in the car for fear the UFO would either kill him or harm him in other ways. There is no way these good people would have both perjured themselves in my presence—no way!

When I pass a lake, I know there is a multitude of life beneath the surface even though I cannot see it. Until a little over one hundred years ago, no one knew there was the minute life form of germs. Until even more recently, even the best scientists in the world didn't know there was an even more minute life form—viruses. There is another life form that exists in another dimension that reveals its presence in different ways. This life form is spiritual in nature. On Cox television, channel 27 (aired in Oklahoma City, May 16, 1996), a documentary on voodoo was presented. Shown on the program was actual footage of voodoo worshipers under the spell of spirit possession, obviously controlled by demons who had taken possession of their bodies and speaking through the ones possessed. In Thailand I have witnessed a female singer with a high soprano voice, accompanying Buddhist temple dancers, suddenly change from a charming girl into a distorted, guttural monkey or snake demon. The voodoo worshippers said they worship two hundred gods, a thousand gods, or innumerable gods.

I cannot say without qualification that UFOs are controlled by good angels or bad angels. I do not know for sure who or what controls them. From biblical light it appears that the only life forms mentioned in Scripture that inhabit the heavens are spiritual, angelic beings also created by God. Therefore, to say that UFOs are angels, fallen or otherwise, is a conclusion, although a reasonable one. The following scriptures present serious questions about angelic travel in the heavenly Kingdom of God:

> The chariots of God are twenty thousand, even thousands of angels: the Lord is among them, as in Sinai, in the holy place (Ps. 68:17).

> And it came to pass, as they still went on, and talked, that, behold, there appeared a chariot of fire, and horses of fire, and parted them both asunder; and Elijah went up by a whirlwind into heaven (2 Kings 2:11).

> For, behold, the LORD will come with fire, and with his chariots like a whirlwind, to render his anger with fury, and his rebuke with flames of fire (Isa. 66:15).

> And I looked, and, behold, a whirlwind came out of the north, a great cloud, and a fire infolding itself, and a brightness was about it, and out of the midst thereof as the colour of amber, out of the midst of the fire. Also out of the midst thereof came the likeness of four

living creatures. And this was their appearance; they had the like-ness of a man. . . . The appearance of the wheels and their work was like unto the colour of a beryl: and they four had one likeness: and their appearance and their work was as it were a wheel in the middle of a wheel (Ezek. 1:4–5,16).

When they had heard the king, they departed; and, lo, the star, which they saw in the east, went before them, till it came and stood over where the young child was (Matt. 2:9).

And, behold, there talked with him two men, which were Moses and Elias. . . . While he thus spake, there came a cloud, and over-shadowed them: and they feared as they entered into the cloud (Luke 9:30,34).

Thinkest thou that I cannot now pray to my Father, and he shall presently give me more than twelve legions of angels? (Matt. 26:53).

According to *Vine's Expository Dictionary of Old and New Testament Words* (p. 200), there are two different words for clouds in the New Testament: *nephos* denotes a cloudy, shapeless mass; *nephele*, the word used in the account of the Transfiguration, the clouds seen by Ezekiel or John, or the cloud over Israel in the wilderness, means something appearing as a cloud with a definite form.

There are hundreds of scriptures that refer to heavenly traffic of angels, chariots of angels, or heavenly lights other than the stars. There are also many references to angels which appear or disappear, indicating they live in a different dimension. It also seems that UFOs likewise appear or disappear at will to certain persons at specific times. I have no opinion as to personal contacts with UFO occupants claimed by some, but this I can testify to: UFOs are real. If they have no relationship to angels—good, bad, or both—then God's Word has left us in darkness, which to me, is unthinkable.

According to a Gallup poll that appeared in the November 20, 1973, edition of the *Daily Oklahoman*, the number of Americans at that time who believed the Earth was being visited by beings from outer space was fifty-one percent. That percentage has not changed. In 1996, according to widely circulated polls, fifty percent of Americans still believe that UFOs are real, with about twenty percent not sure one way or the other. This means that almost twice as many Americans are convinced the Earth is the object of extraterrestrial observation than those who do not.

Far back in time, before the present creation, one of the archangels, Lucifer, purposed to rebel against the Kingdom of God and set up his own kingdom (Ezek. 28:13–18; Isa. 14:12–17). Scripture indicates that one-third of the angels of Heaven followed him. The rebellion of man against God is only a part of the war that has been going on in the heavens (Eph. 6:10–12). In the tenth chapter of Daniel we are given a glimpse of the continuing struggle between the angels of God and the angels of Satan and also of things happening on Earth. God is vitally concerned about what happens to His earthly people, Israel, and Josephus recorded that a strange event happened in the sky over Jerusalem just before the Roman army broke through the wall and destroyed the city.

A few days after that feast, on the one and twentieth day of the month Atemisius, a certain prodigious and incredible phenomenon appeared: I suppose the account of it would seem to be a fable, were it not related by those who saw it, and were not the events that followed it of so considerable a nature as to deserve such signals: for, before sunsetting, chariots and troops of soldiers in their armour were seen running about among the clouds, and surrounding the cities. Moreover, at that feast which we call Pentecost, as the priests were going by night into the inner temple, as their custom was, to perform their sacred ministrations, they said that, in the first place, they felt a quaking, and heard a great noise, and after that they heard a sound as of a great multitude, saying, "Let us remove hence" (*War of the Jews*, Book 6, chapter 5).

We are told that God created Hell for the Devil and his angels (Matt. 25:41), and that ultimate judgment will be carried out when Satan and his army lose the final battle. When this occurs, the angels of God will be under the command of the archangel Michael (Rev. 12:7–9).

If there is an extraterrestrial design behind the construction of pyramid-shaped buildings and related geological phenomena, as many claim, then it would appear that it would be related to the angelic invasion mentioned in Genesis 6:1–2.

We read in Genesis 6:2 that the "sons of God" saw the daughters of men and took wives from among them. The children born of this union were called "giants." Of course, most men see women every day, and men marrying women is the usual and ordinary order of life. But for these "sons of God" to look upon women and marry them was most unusual in that they were angels. We know that Jesus said that the angels of God do not marry, but the angels of Genesis 6 voluntarily left their own estate (Jude 6). We also know that they were angels because Adam is the only man mentioned in the Old Testament as being a son of God. He was a son of God because he was created by God. After Adam sinned, he lost sonship with the Father. Jesus Christ is called "the Son of God" because He was conceived by the Holy Spirit, and only through Jesus Christ are men restored to sonship with God by adoption. Like Adam, angels are called "sons of God" because they are beings by direct creation (Job 1:6; 2:1; 38:7). Some contend that the "sons of God" of Genesis 6 were the sons of Seth, but the late Dr. Clarence Larkin in his book, *The Spirit World*, shows by reference to the original Hebrew that they were angels. Josephus also wrote of them:

> For **many angels of God** accompanied with women, and begat sons that proved unjust, and despisers of all that was good, on account of the confidence they had in their own strength; for the tradition is, that these men did what resembled the acts of those whom the Grecians call giants.

Josephus was one of the most well-educated men of his day, and we can afford him the credit of knowing his own Hebrew language.

God told Moses that the plan for the Tabernacle was patterned after the true Temple in Heaven. Evidence also indicates that the Great Pyramid is of heavenly design. And inasmuch as angels lived on Earth with women before the flood, and children were born of them, it would stand to reason that they would live and construct edifices in accordance with their former estate. Satan is the great counterfeiter because all he knows are the things of God, with which he was formally associated. He cannot create; he can only imitate. The angels of Genesis 6 and their giant descendants could easily be the builders of the lesser pyramids, plus the ring of other pyramid-shaped buildings around the Earth, the ancient carvings of spaceships, the huge drawings on the plains in South America, the fifty-ton stone statues on Easter Island, the monument at Stonehenge, and all related ancient astronomical phenomena.

Jesus said that the Kingdom of Heaven suffered violence (Matt. 11:12), and monuments of stone bear evidence to that part of which took place between the angels of God and the angels of Satan and which touched the Earth. However, the Great Pyramid has stood through the years as mute evidence that the Kingdom of God is progressing toward a victorious conclusion, when all things will be placed under the authority of the Father's heir, His only begotten Son, the Chief Cornerstone, the Lord Jesus Christ (1 Cor. 15:24–27; Matt 25:31; Rev. 19:16).

Chapter Fourteen

The Pharaoh's Ship and
Signs in the Sun

> If a man die, shall he live again? all the days of my appointed time
> will I wait, till my change come. Thou shalt call, and I will answer
> thee: thou wilt have a desire to the work of thine hands (Job 14:14–
> 15).

It is not so much the question of death that has troubled man
over the centuries, but rather how to obtain the best life after
death. The difficulty in witnessing is not convincing the unsaved
of an afterlife, but rather getting them to accept the way to eternal life as set forth in the Bible. The greatest pronouncement
ever made on the subject of life after death was spoken by Jesus
Christ: "I am the resurrection, and the life: he that believeth in
me, though he were dead, yet shall he live," and , "I am the way,
the truth, and the life" (John 11:25; 14:6).

As we have previously observed, it was not the existence of
God nor a belief in life after death that troubled Cain. It was
how to obtain eternal life while at the same time satisfying the
pride of life and lusts of the flesh. Thus religion by works evolved.
Simple faith in God's promises and the way of atonement has
always degenerated into a complicated system of human works,
with man going his own way in the mistaken belief that his
ways and God's will somehow merge in the far distant future.

The simple expression of faith in God's promised Redeemer manifested in the Tabernacle were changed over the years to a complicated religion of works in which every movement and expression of the priests and Levites were governed by some religious intent, even down to tithing the leaves on mint plants. But Jesus Christ said of the adherents to this religious system: "Ye are of your father the devil . . ." (John 8:44). The opposition of man's works to God's way can also be seen in the various denominations during these last days. The doctrine of the preachers of today is the "social gospel" which can be summed up thus: If there is strife in any quarter, doctor up the social order.

The faith of the Egyptians of the first dynasty in burying their dead in a prenatal position was changed into the most elaborate mode of religion ever embraced by a nation, race, or civilization. Quoting from a *Newsweek* article entitled, "The Pyramids and Sphinx":

> The slow deterioration of their position attached the Egyptians more firmly than ever to the god of the afterworld. It was a changing attachment, reflected in a change of artistic styles. Until the nineteenth dynasty, life was probably pleasant for most Egyptians much of the time; hence in their mortuary art they attempted to charm death by vivid representations of physical life. Dancing girls, singing reapers, sailors reaching port, hunters chasing game—such images of a delightful, even joyous mortality are among the images of eternity as well. . . . It became gloomily obsessed with death, with mummification, and with postmortem trials. The underworld and its denizens are shown in lurid carmine and black. According to historian John A. Wilson, this joyous talkative people with "no more fear of death than the fear of walking in a familiar place in the dark" developed into a taciturn, gloomy people whose lot in this world was so grim that every effort, every puritan sacrifice was worthwhile in order to secure something more pleasant in the life to come. It was no longer

a question of eternalizing the joyful moment. The aim was to escape from momentary toils to an eternal improvement, at whatever price in austerity and self-control.

On the south side of the Great Pyramid a huge vault was constructed and lined with granite, with the lid being made of one gigantic slab of granite, approximately fifty feet long, twenty feet wide, and one foot thick. Again, we are once more amazed beyond imagination that such a massive stone could have been moved from southern Egypt, almost five hundred miles distance, to this location. Even today this would be a difficult task, much less forty-five hundred years ago.

When archaeologists finally opened this vault, they discovered an ancient Egyptian ship, almost five thousand years old, still in perfect condition. The rope for the riggings appeared much like the rope available today at the hardware store, and still in almost perfect condition. A picture of the ship, which I took at the museum especially built for this vessel, is in the picture section. I have visited this museum twice, and it is still difficult for me to believe that Cheops sailed on the Nile in this ship. It has been worth the five dollar fee (the cost of a ticket) to go through the Pharaoh's Ship Museum.

No people on Earth ever worked so hard to prepare for life after death, and possibly no people ever came so close to succeeding. We quote from the May 13, 1974, edition of *National Close-up*:

A 27-year-old California scientist believes he may have found the ancient secret of prolonging life. Pat Flanagan is a genius. He is a man of the future. Years ahead of his time. "Death comes about as a result of decay," he says. "History is full of phenomena which may have been caused by biocosmic energy. Examples are the Egyptian mummies, the biblical Ark of the Covenant, and the story of

Methuselah who lived 969 years. . . . Biocosmic energy is the very essence of the life force itself. . . . This energy has been known to exist but until now no one has been able to isolate it. The Great Pyramid of Giza is at last revealed to the world for its true purpose, a very powerful source of biocosmic energy." Fact 1: The word pyramid means literally "Fire in the Middle." Fact 2: In March 1963, biologists of the University of Oklahoma confirmed that the skin cells of the Egyptian princess Meme were capable of living. Fact 3: The princess, needless to say, has been dead for several thousand years.

The mummification of the Egyptian dead can be compared to the modern fantasy of freezing the dead in hope of a future scientific discovery that will restore them to life. Like the mummies, the frozen dead have the capability of life; yet the words of Jesus return to mock all who have attempted to attain life beyond death by some other means:

> . . . I go and prepare a place for you, I will come again, and receive you unto myself; that where I am, there ye may be also. . . . I am the way, the truth and the life: no man cometh unto the Father, but by me (John 14:3,6).

In Scripture, nine is the number of judgment. Jesus Christ died for the sins of the world at the ninth hour. The northern kingdom fell in the ninth year of Josiah's rule. There are nine different accounts of stoning in the Bible. There are nine people mentioned who were afflicted with blindness. The bottomless pit is mentioned nine times. Solomon's Temple and Herod's Temple were both destroyed on the ninth day of Av (August). President Nixon resigned from the presidency of the United States at the end of the most publicized political scandal in the history of the world on the ninth of August. The relation of the number nine to our study of the Great Pyramid is that the ninth plague of God on Egypt was a darkness over the land for three days. This was a total darkness, a darkness so thick it could be felt (Exod. 10:21–23).

At about the time of the Exodus, there was a tremendous volcanic eruption on the island of Thera, renamed Santorini. This eruption was quite similar to the explosion at Krakatoa that sent tidal waves from Indonesia to South America.

The center of Thera disappeared, leaving a ring in the ocean about three miles in diameter. On one side of the circle there is an opening for ships to enter, treating the tourist to a fantastic sight of cliffs hundreds of feet high. When we first visited Santorini we rode mules up stone steps to the top of the city, perched perilously on the rim named Atlantis. Later, cable cars were installed.

When Thera blew its top, the capitol of the Minoan civilization on Crete to the south was buried under a monstrous tidal wave. Even so, the remains of Knossis reveal advanced knowledge in 1400 B.C. of plumbing, hot and cold running water, and the ability to naturally air condition buildings. Even though the temperature outside may be over 100 degrees Fahrenheit, inside the king's palace the temperature is cool and pleasant.

In the northern half of Egypt, including the Cairo area, a layer of volcanic ash, one to three inches deep, dating to 1400 B.C., has been discovered. It has been suggested that the volcanic eruption of Thera occurred at the time of the Exodus, and a strong north wind blew the volcanic ash over much of Egypt, which accounted for the description of the ninth plague as being so dark it could be felt. Whether this was the exact cause of the darkness is not a matter of concern because regardless what caused it, God was in control.

All of the judgments against Egypt were meant to reveal to Pharaoh that the God of Moses was greater than all of his gods.

Each judgment was against a god whom the Egyptians worshipped, the principal one being Ra, the sun god. The ninth
plague showed that the God of Moses was more powerful than
the most exalted deity of the Pharaoh.

The sun god Ra (or Re) is dated before the flood, from the
second dynasty onward. In the fifth dynasty, a new name appeared in the Egyptian temples—"Sa-Ra," meaning the "son of
Ra." The entire sun god concept was a satanic attempt to divert
men from the hope of the coming true Redeemer, God's only
begotten Son. It is entirely possible that "Sa-Ra" was a son born
to one of the angels mentioned in Genesis 6:2. We read in "Pyramids and Sphinx" in *Newsweek* that Ra was the "chief deity of
the pyramid builders." His image and religious praises are inscribed in all the tombs and pyramids of Egypt; all, that is, except the Great Pyramid. Ra was the spirit who inspired the Egyptians to build monuments to the heavens, and the solar ships
enclosed in the tombs were designed to carry the dead to eternal habitation with Ra in the sun. Contrarily, the Great Pyramid, in its astronomical and mathematical calculations, presents
the sun as nothing more than a heavenly body, the center of our
solar system, a creation of God. Thus the calculations of the
pyramid relative to the sun are in perfect harmony with science
and the Word of God.

Without giving too many scientific details, we introduce evidence concerning the sun, both from Scripture and science, to
show again that the Great Pyramid alone of all the pyramids in
the world reveals a Divine architect. Moses wrote in Genesis
1:14–19 that the heavenly bodies were not only made for light,
but for signs—that is, prophecy. Jesus said of His return: "And
there shall be signs in the sun, and in the moon, and in the
stars" (Luke 21:25). The prophet Joel said:

And I will shew wonders in the heavens and in the earth, blood, and fire, and pillars of smoke. The sun shall be turned into darkness, and the moon into blood, before the great and the terrible day of the LORD come (Joel 2:30-31).

Joel said that men would be given two great signs that the Lord's return was near—a sign in the Earth and wonders in the sun. The sign in the Earth would be pillars of smoke rising up from fire and blood. In an atomic explosion, fire and blood are mingled and then a great pillar of smoke rises up thousands of feet into the atmosphere. The Bible declares that when you see this happening you will know that the coming of the Lord is near.

The second sign would be a great wonder in the sun. Of course, we understand that there are scores of end-time signs being fulfilled before our eyes, but the reference here is to a visible sign that men and women all over the Earth could see with the naked eye.

Sunspots, which are great nuclear explosions on the sun, are becoming more frequent and more extensive. In an Associated Press news release dated May 6, 1974, the Goddard Space Flight Center in New York is quoted as saying that a solar explosion on the sun on August 4, 1972, lengthened the day ten times more than was expected at that time of the year. A United Press International release of July 6, 1974, reported a gigantic solar storm covering an area as large as the planet Jupiter, some 1.1 billion square miles.

The Bible has much to say about the sun as a prophetic instrument to warn men to prepare for the judgments of the Great Tribulation:

. . . the light of the moon shall be as the light of the sun, and the light of the sun shall be sevenfold, as the light of seven days, in the day that the LORD bindeth up the breach of his people, and healeth the stroke of their wound (Isa. 30:26).

And the fourth angel poured out his vial upon the sun; and power was given unto him to scorch men with fire. And men were scorched with great heat, and blasphemed the name of God, which hath power over these plagues: and they repented not to give him glory (Rev. 16:8–9).

And I will shew wonders in the heavens and in the earth, blood, and fire, and pillars of smoke. The sun shall be turned into darkness, and the moon into blood, before the great and the terrible day of the LORD come (Joel 2:30–31).

Immediately after the tribulation of those days shall the sun be darkened, and the moon shall not give her light . . . (Matt. 24:29).

Isaiah and John said that the sun would become bright and hot, but Jesus and Joel said it would be darkened when the Lord comes. However, there is no contradiction. Any astronomer knows that when a star novas—and our sun is an average star— it heats up, becomes unusually bright for 7 to 10 days, and then goes dark. Scientists have predicted in the past that the sun would last another ten billion years because only half of its hydrogen supply has been used. But Dr. Iosef S. Shklovsky, of the Shtenberg State Astronomical Institute in Moscow, calculated that when the sun's hydrogen supply drops to forty-nine percent and the helium content increases to fifty-one percent, it will expand and heat up to more than one hundred times its present temperature.

If, as some have speculated, our sun is approaching a critical balance between helium and hydrogen, then it could nova at any time. Large stars bigger than our sun supernova in a monstrous nuclear explosion. Three supernovas are seen each year in just our galaxy, the Milky Way. In a nova a star's atoms are stripped of their shells and then the entire mass collapses into a ball, perhaps no more than fifteen miles in diameter, where the gravity is so intense no light can escape. According to the Kirkpatrick Planetarium in Oklahoma City, there are at least thirty novas each year within our galaxy.

The Egyptians, in building their tombs, manifested faith that the sun god would save them, rather than relying on the God who not only created the sun but all things in Heaven and in Earth. The Great Pyramid points to the passing away of all lights, except the light of God in Jesus Christ, which will shine upon the redeemed for all eternity:

> For, behold, the day cometh, that shall burn as an oven; and all the proud, yea, and all that do wickedly, shall be stubble: and the day that cometh shall burn them up, saith the LORD of hosts, that it shall leave them neither root nor branch. But unto you that fear my name shall the Sun of righteousness arise with healing in his wings . . . (Mal. 4:1-2).

Inasmuch as several Bible scholars who have studied the Great Pyramid thought that Enoch was the architect, would not this antediluvian patriarch have incorporated all this knowledge of things to come into its construction? Surely he would have. According to Josephus, the Great Pyramid was to endure throughout the ages until the judgment of the Tribulation fires. God is not willing that any should perish in this coming judgment (2 Pet. 3:9). The great increase of knowledge in these last days has made possible the unlocking of the secrets of the Great Pyramid, as well as the use of radio and television to broadcast the gospel into all nations, and the publishing of the Word in books and tracts to afford the widest dissemination possible. Never in the history of the world has mankind been given such a universal invitation to accept Jesus Christ as Lord and Savior and be saved. Christ is knocking at the door of the hearts of millions right now, including the heart of the reader if he or she is unsaved.

In benediction, we pray that this brief study will be a blessing to thousands, helping them to better prepare for the return of the Lord, before whom we must all appear to give an account of the deeds done in the flesh (Rom. 14:10–12).

And to those who do not know Jesus Christ personally, we pray that the evidence compiled in this book will help convince them that He is indeed the Son of God and the only means by which man's sins can be forgiven and fellowship with God the Father restored. If but one person receives Christ through the ministry of this book, its purpose will have been achieved.

Two fishermen at early light run their lines in the Nile to retrieve their meager catch. Since the construction of the Aswan Dam, the number and size of fish in the Nile has steadily declined.

The one-hundred–square-mile City of the Dead in the Cairo area. Lepers live in many of the tombs today.

A donkey provides the power for an irrigation pump to draw water from a canal that branches off the Nile. Seen in the background is one of the step pyramids of Sakkara.

The largest step pyramid at Sakkara. These were lesser pyramids requiring few construction skills. A layer of stone was laid (mustafa) and then another was laid upon it, etc.

Outer walls and entrance to one of the buildings housing the tombs of Sakkara. Simplistic but artistic design is copied by even contemporary architecture.

Pillars supporting the roof to one of the ancient temples at Sakkara demonstrate a superior culture whose knowledge of construction and mathematics antedated that of the Greeks by two thousand years.

The Pyramid of Menkaure, the smallest of the three at Giza. The keyhole appearance of the opening is probably the result of tomb robbers trying to find treasure.

The entrance to the Great Pyramid that was hidden for over three thousand years.

Kim Hutchings (wife of author) stands beside one of the building blocks to show comparative size. One of the few remaining limestone casing blocks is evident at the bottom of the picture.

The Sphinx of Giza with the body of a lion and the head of a man (or some believe a woman) was partially made of brick, but the head is made of stone. It is 187 feet long, and some believe it represents the zodiac.

The nose of the Sphinx has been marred by gunfire, charged to soldiers in Napoleon's army. Other historical notes disagree. Vertical erosion marks indicate it was constructed when water was abundant. Josephus seems to indicate that both the Sphinx and the pyramids were erected before the flood.

The pyramid complex of Giza as seen from a distance. From right to left, the pyramids of Khufu (Cheops), Khafre, and Menkaure. Although the pyramid of Khafre appears to be the largest, it is built on a higher level and is dwarfed by the Great Pyramid.

Staff Photo

Staff Photo

An overview of the Valley of the Kings where excavations are still in progress. These are ornate tombs, some extending into the mountain for several hundred feet. The latest tomb (discovered in 1995) contained at least fifty mummies of the sons of Ramses II.

The dogs of Egypt usually just lie in the shade to escape the heat. It is said that Egyptian dogs do not bark, because God closed their mouths when Israel departed at the Exodus (Exod. 11:7).

Entrance to one of the very few Coptic churches in Egypt. As in most predominantly Islamic nations, any church or assembly identified as Christian must keep a low profile or suffer persecution. Egypt is 94 percent Muslim.

Egyptian children from ages six to ten work in rug weaving establishments or other plants to learn a trade and make a few extra pennies a day to help support their families.

Children in one of the many ghettos of Cairo. It is in these slums that Islamic fanatics work to recruit revolutionaries and terrorists.

Downtown Cairo during one of the off-rush hours. During traffic peaks, the streets are congested with millions of cars. Cairo, formerly Siriad, now rivals New York City, Mexico City, and Shanghai in population.

Chapter Fifteen

The Pyramid in Space

On our first visit to the museum of King Cheops' Royal Solar Ship in 1983, we obtained a copy of *The Boat Beneath the Pyramid*, a book concerning this 1,224-piece vessel that was first uncovered in 1954. We quote from this book:

> More than a quarter of a century ago a young Egyptian archaeologist, clearing a site just south of the Great Pyramid of Giza, broke through a massive slab of limestone to reveal a deep vault beneath his feet. For the first time in 4,500 years the sun's rays were shining down on the timbers of a great cedarwood ship, built for a king, and then dismantled and buried here at the height of the Egyptian Old Kingdom. Astonishingly well preserved, it was by far the most ancient vessel ever to come to light.

The workmen who prepared and sealed the vault evidently had the amazing technology to store it in such a way that it would not deteriorate. We quote from pages 166–67 of the book, *The Boat Beneath the Pyramid*:

> "The wooden parts of the boat," wrote the late Dr. Abdel Moneium Abubakr in 1971, "were as hard and new as if they had been placed there but a year ago." Kamal El-Mallakh recalls that when he opened the pit in 1954 the original color of the wood was warm and light and "so highly polished that I could sometimes see my own reflection in a piece of side planking."

The ship itself evidenced excellent workmanship and is about eighty feet long and twelve feet wide. The knowledge and technology that existed four and a half millennia ago to build and preserve the ship is almost as astounding as that which went into the construction of the Great Pyramid. The author of *The Boat Beneath the Pyramid*, Nancy Jenkins, surmised on page 45:

> Everything that could be known about the Great Pyramid was known, it seemed, except for the still-puzzling question of how a society whose technology had not yet arrived at the wheel, was able to erect such a massive structure in the first place.

Besides the pyramids at Giza, there are many other pyramids built by ancient civilizations circling the equatorial regions of Earth. All of these pyramids have had religious significance to their builders, and many in Central and South America built by Incas, Mayans, and Aztecs, indicate they were used as observatories. Their builders knew about the equinoxes, the movement of the planets, and the knowledge of computing solar time. Why or how did these ancients incorporate such knowledge of the heavens in pyramidal-shaped structures that were thousands of years in advance of their time?

The Sphinx, about one-half mile from the Great Pyramid, signifies the precision of the equinoxes, the travel of the sun through the constellations of our galaxy, a time period of 25,827 years.

The moon orbits (or circles) the Earth every twenty-eight days. The Earth and moon circle the sun every three hundred and sixty-five days. The sun and all its planets circle the center of the Milky Way galaxy every 25,827 years (if time has extended, or will extend that long). When man thought the Earth was flat and the sun was a god, we read in the first book of the Bible to be written, that the Creator "walketh in the circuit of heaven"

(Job 22:14). It has been supposed that the Sphinx united the first sign and the last sign on the astrological chart representing the precession of the constellations. However, in ancient cultures such figures were in Greece, Assyria, and other countries. They represented guardians. The Sphinx of Egypt near the Great Pyramid has the body of a lion and the head of a Pharaoh. The head was probably carved in the likeness of the Pharaoh at that time.

It has been a common belief that the Sphinx dated to the eleventh to fifteenth dynasty. However, Piazzi Smyth offered evidence that it could be as old as the Great Pyramid, or even older (page 508, *The Great Pyramid*). Archaeological inspections of the Sphinx in 1994–95 seem to verify Smyth's conclusion. The lion section of the Sphinx, according to a television production hosted by Charlton Heston, was originally made of bricks. Stone was later used in the remodeling process, and the head of a Pharaoh added much later, possibly as late as the fifteenth dynasty. The older section of the Sphinx evidenced water erosion. Wind erosion leaves horizontal lines, but the erosion evidenced in the Sphinx is vertical, indicating water. Therefore the Sphinx was originally constructed before the flood, or in a time when rain was common to the area. Could the Sphinx be the monument in Siriad (Cairo) erected of bricks by the sons of Seth referred to by Josephus?

In Genesis 2:11–14 Moses wrote that in the Garden of Eden there was a river with four tributaries: Pison, Gihon, Hiddekel, and Euphrates. It would seem that the Gihon would be the Nile as this river went through Ethiopia, or it could be that the Gihon dried up. To the west of Egypt through the Libyan desert, beneath the sand, lies the river bed of a once great river. In any event, the four tributaries of the river in Eden were broken off and separated when the continents broke off the one large land mass. This happened after the flood in the days of Peleg (Gen.

10:25). Geologists, almost without exception, have concluded that hundreds of thousands of years, or millions of years, were required for the continents and islands to separate and move to their present locations. However, now there is a new and revolutionary concept that the separation of the land mass into continents occurred quite suddenly, possibly within days. Supportive evidence of this opinion are tree stumps and petrified wood in deserts, palm trees preserved in ice at the North Pole, and grass in the stomachs of mammoths at the Arctic Circle. It has been reported that Eskimos have actually thawed out these mammoths to feed to their sled dogs. Certainly, this change that suddenly froze huge animals could not have occurred over months, years, or millenniums. It had to have occurred suddenly. While science cannot provide answers to these many perplexing questions, we can accept as fact that nothing in archaeology, geology, or the written history of man contradicts anything within the sixty-six books of the Bible.

The present generation has looked to space for answers to mysteries of Earth's past. The United States' explorations to the moon have resulted in detailed photographs of Earth's lunar satellite. These, as well as astronauts landing on the moon, have uncovered nothing that could not, to at least some satisfaction, be scientifically explained. However, the only two planets where satellites have landed and taken pictures are Venus and Mars. Satellite findings from Venus reveal a surface temperature of 800 degrees Fahrenheit, clouds that rain sulfuric acid, intense gravity, and with vapors limiting photographic vision. Because of the environment, satellites that have landed on Venus have been shortlived and only a few pictures have been transmitted.

The surface of Mars, as taken by cameras in NASA satellites, indicate that it was once a living planet. The dry riverbeds indicate a previous abundance of water. We quote from *Catalogue of the Universe*:

> If once great cities stood here [Mars], they have crumbled to unrecognizable shapes. If trees bowed before the moist zephyrs, they have returned to the dust whence they rose. If aircraft landed here, they too have vanished, or been buried beneath unknown depths of sand and rocks. There is no life here. The soil is richly capable of supporting life as we know it, given water.

s reported in the *Encyclopedia of Space Travel and Astronomy*, several experiments conducted by NASA satellites on Mars' surface determine if there was animal or vegetable life at any time on the planet were inconclusive. Some indicated that there was at one time life on Mars, and others indicated the response could have been due to chemical action.

PM Magazine, a 30-minute daily television program formerly produced in Oklahoma City and heard locally over channel 4, carried a segment concerning a report by Vincent Di Pietro, a technician at NASA. Mr. Di Pietro had read in a UFO magazine about the *Viking* satellite probe of Mars taking pictures of a huge stone face with a large pyramid in the vicinity. This program was telecast December 26, 1983. Mr. Di Pietro, thinking to prove his report to be a complete hoax, reviewed the Viking film series of Mars in the NASA film library. To his astonishment, the pictures were real and have since been reported in a NASA publication, #76H593, 72nd frame. We quote from Vincent Di Pietro's book, *Unusual Martian Surface Features*:

> A long time has passed since I saw that remarkable picture of a face on Mars. It was 1977 and the photograph was made from the *Viking* spacecraft orbiting the planet Mars, at least that is what the caption said. At first I did not believe it. I thought it might be a hoax or some fictitious image made by a movie studio doing a science fiction movie. . . . The second picture also revealed a monstrous rectangular pyramid (one mile by 1.6 miles). A further peculiarity is that there ap-

pears to be four sides that go down to the surface at sharp angles. The corners exhibit symmetrical material, almost as if they were being buttressed.

The amazing thing about the *Viking* pictures is that the pyramid on the surface of Mars appears to be much like the Great Pyramid of Giza, and the face on Mars looks very much like the face of the Sphinx. While one side of the face was shown to be in the shadows, a computer-enhanced photograph brought out the full features, showing two perfect eyes with even the eyeballs perfectly formed, two nostrils, full lips, and chin. NASA technicians say they cannot explain how this could have happened by chance.

There are also other mysterious formations and objects revealed in the Martian photographs, including one called "Inca City," because of its strange resemblance to the ancient abandoned Incan cities in Peru and Bolivia. No one has ever satisfactorily explained the huge figures and areas that appear to be ancient landing strips on the plains at Nazca. We cannot help but wonder if there is not some connection between the pyramid and the face that looks like that of the Sphinx on Mars with the solar ship, the Sphinx, and the Great Pyramid at Giza.

It is a belief of some scientists that a great catastrophe rocked our solar system approximately ten thousand years ago. If this be true, then we can attribute it to the war in Heaven when Lucifer, an archangel who had dominion over one-third of the universe, decided to take over the entire Kingdom of God. We read in Isaiah 14:12–13:

How art thou fallen from heaven, O Lucifer, son of the morning! how art thou cut down to the ground, which didst weaken the nations! For thou hast said in thine heart, I will ascend into heaven, I will exalt my throne above the stars of God: I will sit also upon the mount of the congregation, in the sides of the north.

Further insight into the Devil's present activities is given in Ezekiel 28:17–18:

> Thine heart was lifted up because of thy beauty, thou hast corrupted thy wisdom by reason of thy brightness: I will cast thee to the ground, I will lay thee before kings, that they may behold thee. Thou hast defiled thy sanctuaries by the multitude of thine iniquities, by the iniquity of thy traffick; therefore will I bring forth a fire from the midst of thee, it shall devour thee, and I will bring thee to ashes upon the earth in the sight of all them that behold thee.

Since the time of his decision to take over the universe, this angelic rebel has been creating havoc in the galaxies with his demonic traffic. There has been continuing war in the heavens, and the final war is described in Revelation 12:7–8:

> And there was war in heaven: Michael and his angels fought against the dragon; and the dragon fought and his angels, And prevailed not; neither was their place found any more in heaven.

Some scientists conclude that there is evidence of war in heaven today. We quote from an article entitled, "Aliens in Outer Space Fighting Real-Life Star Wars," by Malcolm J. Nicholl:

> Real-life "Star Wars" are raging in outer space! Top scientists believe that mysterious explosions in deep space—which resemble high nuclear blasts—are the result of alien beings locked in a furious intergalactic war. "Frankly, I can't help feeling that there is some sort of intergalactic warfare going on that we have detected," declared William Gould, a spacecraft manager at the government's Goddard Space Flight Center. Dr. Willard P. Armstrong—a space authority and a retired professor of chemical engineering at Washington University—said, "I feel sure the explosions are caused by super races involved in star wars." The latest and most violent blast hurtled through

168 ◆ The Great Pyramid

space on March 5 and was detected by eight widely scattered space probes, including three American satellites on patrol to detect bursts of radiation from sneak nuclear weapons tests. In the last ten years there have been at least eighty similar unexplained explosions in deep space. Stunned scientists have ruled out the possibility that the powerful explosions are natural space phenomena known as super-novas. . . . Houston-based space specialist James Oberg said, "It is a reasonable suggestion by some other scientists that the blasts are being caused by intelligent life forms. It is a legitimate theory that 'star wars' may be taking place." Top engineering physicist Dr. Henry Monteith—who works for the prestigious Sandia Laboratory in Albuquerque, New Mexico, and who has been studying space phenomena for twenty years—declared: "It's possible a mysterious happening like this could well be something as exotic as a space war."

If there is a nuclear war at the present time in outer space, as these scientists concur, then we can be sure it is the continuing war that has been going on for millennia between the angels of God and the angels of Satan. At the present time, the chief concern of the major powers on Earth is that mankind will enter the "star wars" conflict.

We quote from an article in the December 17, 1984, edition of *U.S. News and World Report* entitled, "Space-War Era—It's Already Here":

Far from being a futuristic science-fiction fantasy, the militarization of space already is happening at a quiet but rapidly accelerating pace high above the planet. So advanced is the military thrust into space, say experts, that the heavens would be a crucial battleground if war were to erupt tomorrow between the Soviet Union and the United States. . . . "Our space systems have become essential to our operational forces," explains Air Force Under-Secretary Edward Aldridge. "We're going to have to defend them." . . . "Even in a very limited war, we would have an absolutely critical dependence on space today," says White House science advisor George Keyworth. "Survivability of our space assets is one of our most important priorities." Already some eight percent of American military communications are transmitted by satellites—in many cases the only links between senior authorities in Washington and commanders in the field, ship captains at sea, pilots in the air. . . . The Soviet Union, which started experimenting with lasers and particle beams on a large scale earlier than the United States, may become the first to put up an orbiting battle station. . . . But regardless of the arguments over the wisdom of an extraterrestrial-arms contest, few experts seriously expect that the militarization of space will be reversed anytime soon, either through superpower arms negotiations or domestic political and economical pressures. Once the high ground of the heavens is seized, neither side is likely to give it up readily.

Since 1984 the Soviet Union has disintegrated and the Reagan administration's "Star Wars" project has for the most part been abandoned. However, a new weapon, possibly even more dangerous, has replaced the old ones. In 1986 I wrote a paper on the possible future use of extreme low frequency (ELF) radio wave transmissions as a mind control and weather weapon. Ten years later, in 1996, such a system is being installed north of Anchorage, Alaska. The government project is called HAARP (High-frequency Active Auroral Research Project). According to a book by Dr. Nick Begich, *Angels Don't Play This HAARP*, this could be the ultimate "star wars" weapon. By sending millions of watts of ELF radio waves into the ground and air, using three hundred transmitters, it might be possible to change weather, confuse mental processes, x-ray the entire Earth, totally destroy communications systems, and even destroy missiles and satellites. Meanwhile, nuclear proliferation continues, and men and nations still cry peace, peace, but there is no peace.

According to God's Word, Satan is maneuvering the nations of Earth to engage in a space war to destroy them. According to Josephus, the Great Pyramid of Giza contained knowledge of the heavens and a warning to mankind that the Earth would, at the end of the age, be destroyed by fire.

Never before has the prophecy of the Apostle Peter recorded in his second epistle, chapter 3:7–13, become so important for mankind. It is more relevant than the words of all the diplomats in the world voiced at Geneva, or any other peace conference which is governed by the wisdom of men:

> But the heavens and the earth, which are now, by the same word are kept in store, reserved unto fire against the day of judgment and perdition of ungodly men. But, beloved, be not ignorant of this one thing, that one day is with the Lord as a thousand years, and a thousand years as one day. The Lord is not slack concerning his promise, as some men count slackness; but is longsuffering to us-ward, not willing that any should perish, but that all should come to repentance. But the day of the Lord will come as a thief in the night; in the which the heavens shall pass away with a great noise, and the elements shall melt with fervent heat, the earth also and the works that are therein shall be burned up. Seeing then that all these things shall be dissolved, what manner of persons ought ye to be in all holy conversation and godliness, Looking for and hasting unto the coming of the day of God, wherein the heavens being on fire shall be dissolved, and the elements shall melt with fervent heat? Nevertheless we, according to his promise, look for new heavens and a new earth, wherein dwelleth righteousness.

When Jesus Christ entered Jerusalem His disciples went before Him praising God: "Blessed be the King that cometh in the name of the Lord: peace in heaven, and glory in the highest."

When the unbelievers protested, Jesus responded: "I tell you that, if these should hold their peace, the stones would immediately cry out."

There does seem to be a story in the Great Pyramid, a type of the New Jerusalem. The stones do cry out that the King is coming; the glory of the Lord will fill the Earth, and there will be peace in Heaven.

However, the great cornerstone will fall upon those whose names are not written in the Lamb's Book of Life. The missing capstone on the Great Pyramid speaks to us of Luke 20:17–18:

> . . . What is this then that is written, The stone which the builders rejected, the same is become the head of the corner? Whosoever shall fall upon that stone shall be broken; but on whomsoever it shall fall, it will grind him to powder.

According to Daniel 2:44, this great stone will then fill all the world and the prophetic purpose of the Great Pyramid will then be fulfilled.

NOAH HUTCHINGS is president of Southwest Radio Ministries, one of the foremost prophetic ministries in the world. He has written dozens of books and booklets on prophecy and other Bible themes. Pastor Hutchings has been active in missions and communications ministries for more than 50 years, and has led mission tours to Israel, Egypt, Europe, China, Russia, and other nations around the world. His plain and conversational style of writing makes the subject matter he approaches both interesting and informative to the reader, regardless of the level of education or understanding.

REVELATION FOR TODAY

The book of Revelation is the most misunderstood of all the 66 books of the Bible. The reason is that the events prophesied in this book were not possible until the present generation. This verse-by-verse study will give the reader a new understanding of this exciting book.

224 pages   ♦   8½ x 11   ♦   ISBN 0-9744764-4-7

DANIEL THE PROPHET

This is an insightful study of the life, times, and prophecies of Daniel. This book is a comprehensive examination of the prophecies concerning the historical and future gentile world empires.

336 pages   ♦   ISBN 1-57558-032-2

U.S. IN PROPHECY

U.S. in Prophecy presents an appraisal and hopefully objective conclusion that considers all the facts and evidence as relating to the United States as the Babylon of Revelation 18.

240 pages   ♦   ISBN 0-9744764-9-8

PETRA IN HISTORY AND PROPHECY

Petra is the most amazing ghost town in the world and, we believe, Israel's hiding place during the last half of the tribulation. This is a fascinating book about coming events; and, it will be a witness to Israel, both now and during the coming time of Jacob's trouble.

240 pages   ♦   Full-Color Photographs   ♦   ISBN 0-9744764-9-8